Evans Modern Teaching

Parent-teacher Partnership

Evans Modern Teaching

Parent-teacher Partnership

Graham Bond

Headmaster, Marshlands Primary School, Sussex

Evans Brothers Limited   London

Published by Evans Brothers Limited
Montague House
Russell Square, London WC1

Filmset in 10 on 11pt Imprint by
Thomson Litho, East Kilbride, Scotland,
and printed in Great Britain by
T. & A. Constable Ltd., Edinburgh.

ISBN 0 237 28620 3   PRA 3191

Contents

Introduction

'Parents and teachers are natural enemies, predestined each for the discomforture of the other.' So wrote Willard Waller in his book *The Sociology of Teaching*.

Dr Michael Young, writing in *Linking Home and School*, said 'Some teachers seem to be afraid of parents, sometimes of the hefty father who roars into the school to complain of some imagined maltreatment of his child, more often of the busybody who is thought to want to interfere in things the teacher thinks are outside the province of the parent. How often in conversation is the horror of the American parent-teacher association invoked.'

It is from these two starting points (that are unfortunately not at all uncommon) that it is intended to describe some ways out of these sad, defensive states.

Since the publication of the Plowden Report, *Children and their Primary Schools,* with its central theme of the need for real home and school relationships and direct practical parent-teacher partnership (not just co-operation or association), the debates and writings have been extensive and far-ranging. Unfortunately, however, it appears that these discussions have so often been divorced from the realities of the situation. The readiest example is of course the oft-quoted bogy of the American PTA about which Plowden wrote and to which further reference will be made based on mine and many others' experiences.

As so often happens, it is the overworked class teacher who has been denied the chance of a reasonably detailed consideration of the research findings or case studies which are now in existence. Teachers do find time for an amazing amount of work in building up their resources and extending their expertise, but by the nature of their work schedules, priorities have to be decided upon. It is not really surprising that they receive little encouragement at any level to make this whole area of home and school relationships a priority. More often than not, all teachers (heads included) only read snippet or 'sniping' reviews of books and research digests or hear the 'to the barricades' speeches by some of the Union or Association spokesmen, who practically always have taken up defensive postures when parent-teacher matters are 'news'. Frequently, of course, it is the extremist statement and the exceptional (in the bad sense) incidents which receive the publicity through the various news media. The countless positive contributions and examples of good and profitable practice are not considered 'newsworthy'.

Is it to be wondered at, therefore, that we still have a very long way to go before parents and teachers are really communicating with each other and working in active partnership for the educational growth of their children?

When sociologists can be quoted in support of the non-involvement of parents in the schools' work programme, this naturally reinforces the lazy, diffident or complacent head to take no initiative in these matters. For, to be perfectly fair, if a sociologist writes to the effect that 'some empirical evidence suggests that closer contacts may produce differences as well as resolve them' and when Professor Philip H. Taylor says that 'residual conflict between home and school is inevitable and may not even be a bad thing', unless you are a very determined individual you are likely to proceed no further. For a further exposition of these, and similar viewpoints, readers are referred to a paper by T. Parsons, *The School Class as a Social System and Some of its Functions in American Society*, published in the autumn 1969 number of the *Harvard Educational Review*.

What, however, I think is important to understand from the very beginning, is that many of us have been actively working with parents for over a quarter of a century (and exceptional men like George Lyward for over half a century) and all of this work has been positive and practical and, above all, productive both socially and academically. Great though the work and influence of the Plowden Report has been during these last six years, the build up of attack, or disparagement of its main message that has followed virtually ignores all the good practice and results that have gone before. As will be shown in the following pages, we have a host of authorities, both national and local, who from the 1930s onwards have been stressing the need for the teachers, parents and children to be actively and practically linked for their greater good and mutual aid.

But what we need, it seems, in addition to the backing of authorities and the example of much successful practice, are definite guide lines. In the pages that follow, not only will problems be posed and recognised, but solutions propounded. I am convinced that many teachers are holding back because they have not had either the training (initially or in service) or the experience in this work. Few colleges of education include this in their teacher training programmes and many teachers (six out of every ten) are working in schools which have little or no planned contact with parents.

What, however, have grown up and been accelerated by the publication of the Plowden Report are the several organisations which can be of real help to those who wish to develop this activity within their schools. When this whole scene is surveyed, it is hoped that no teachers will feel this is now a task beyond them, or one which has to be tackled in isolation.

Finally, in these days when 'greater productivity' is the cry which answers wage and salary demands, it might well be that some of the more vocal spokesmen of teachers' unions and associations, who from time to time condemn some aspects of parent-teacher co-operation or involvement, should pause and reflect that here at last is something they could advance as an argument in favour of salary claims! For indeed there is real and substantial research evidence to show that where teachers give time to the encouragement of home and school matters, parental concern and interest develop and children's (*ipso facto* teacher's) 'productivity' increases!

Reasons for teachers attitude.

Acknowledgements

I would like to record my thanks to the parents and teachers of the five schools of which I have been Head for their support, encouragement and ideas. My thanks are also due to my students at Goldsmiths' College, who have made me re-examine closely my ideas on partnership.

G. B.

Chapter 1

The need to understand and
work with parents

The importance of p-t. partnership.
- progress in child (academic).
- Refer to Douglas again

The answer to this basic necessity needs to be considered from the
educational, sociological and psychological angles. What this means to
the class teacher in practical terms is in fact very simple and clear.
As a direct and traceable result of taking parents into partnership, can
we give affirmative answers to all of the following questions?
  Will John and Mary progress more steadily and readily in terms of
their educational attainments? Will they, as Lord Boyle once wrote,
'acquire intelligence and develop their talents and abilities to the full'
more successfully?
  Will John and Mary grow socially and fit more happily and with
some feeling of satisfaction into their environment?
  Will there be less of a traumatic experience on school entry?
  Will John's and Mary's whole personalities be more balanced and
soundly based as a result of this understanding and involvement between
their parents and their teachers?
  The research findings of Dr J. W. B. Douglas, published in his book
The Home and the School, and the National Survey results found in
Appendix 3, Volume 2 of the Plowden Report all give clear and affirmative answers to these questions. But where these are suspect (many people
still repeat the jibe about 'damned statistics') a reader can look closely
at the finely written-up case studies in Patrick McGeeney's books *Parents
are Welcome* and *Learning Begins at Home.*
  While a great deal of material is to be found in all of the chapters
in Douglas's book, it is in Chapter 7 that we read:

'At both eight and eleven years, but particularly at eleven, the highest average scores in the tests are made by children whose parents are most interested in their education and the lowest by those whose parents are least interested. This is partly a social class effect stemming from the large proportions of upper middle-class children among the former and of manual working-class children among the latter. But the relation between the children's scores and their parents' attitudes persists within each social class. It is less marked in the middle classes than in the manual working classes, but it is *substantial* in both and cannot be explained away in terms of social selection alone. In the upper middle-classes, for instance, the children of very interested parents make scores that are 3·7 points higher on average than those made by children of uninterested parents. In the lower manual working class they make scores that are 9·2 points higher.'

From this study we have some positive proof that in all strata of society there will be a real improvement in the academic attainments of boys and girls where the parents take an active interest in the progress and development of their children. In fact, in Dr Douglas's study, the extent of this interest is rather limited, but it is apparently sufficient to make significant measurable differences in attainment. Also, of course, from the yardsticks used perhaps only the tip of the iceberg is revealed. Parents who make the effort to visit the school and talk to the class teacher, and are willing to communicate in other ways, are undoubtedly more likely to be interested and concerned with their child's work and activities generally, within the home situation.

Where, however, the links established are worked at and fostered even further by the school so that all parents know that the school and its teachers are genuinely welcoming, the results in work, attitudes and attainments are even more spectacular and encouraging. These will be schools where opportunities are created, at varying levels, for mother and father to be seen actively working within the school; where it is known that regularly, without fuss and formality (or the lecture pose from the teachers), parents can go into the school in the evening and talk with each other and the teachers and learn about the 'new' maths, science, Nuffield French or art and craft (and have answered the query 'Why do they always seem to be drawing and painting?').

Having cited two sources where the enquiring, or sceptical teacher can go and discover factual evidence based on systematic research, I think it might help to add an example from my own experience.

In a school within an area that would, in socio-economic terms, come within the lower third (the majority of fathers' occupations being unskilled or semi-skilled) we were able still to obtain a large amount of parental co-operation, interest and involvement. Over a period of four years this developed so much that within a school of almost 500 juniors we discovered, as a result of an educational psychologist's investigation, that our genuine problem of very difficult children formed only a quarter of what was said to be the norm for such a school or area. The only significant reason that could be discovered for this fact was that our school was really 'open' and the parents knew that the teachers were approachable and welcoming. We undertook various minor case studies and had some quite dramatic results. One boy, Kenneth, who came to us aged 8·5 years with shocking behaviour reports, and soon lived up to them, became quickly the terror of the probationary teachers and ancillary staff. As a staff we discussed Kenneth thoroughly and then brought the parents into a 'conference' between the class teacher and myself. The rest of the staff were kept fully informed of all that we learned and how we intended to proceed. By this very necessary step it meant that Kenneth was less likely to be treated differently by each one of us if he happened to run foul of any of us. The father, who like many was a shift worker, agreed somewhat reluctantly at first to come in during one working session each week when he was on the appropriate shift. All we suggested was that he came in and walked all round the school, seeing what was going on everywhere and then having a talk with Kenneth's teacher. It was, of course, vital that the teacher felt comfortable about this and we saw to it that there was always something special to show the father. We also often saved up some small suitable 'chore' which the class teacher, somewhat diffidently, would ask if he could possibly manage for us.

Over the period of a term the improvement in Kenneth's behaviour was very noticeable. At the end of the year he was literally a changed boy from the character who had almost produced terror. Kenneth was co-operative, friendly and working well and of course, as a result, his reading age and output of work increased considerably.

Several other similar cases could be given, where as a direct result of one or both parents being brought in on a working partnership basis the problems and difficulties were largely overcome.

But to achieve these kind of results it is not only the parents who have to feel accepted as equal partners but all the staff of the school. It is not without significance that the most hierarchical and authoritarian school set-ups are the ones with virtually non-existent worthwhile parent-teacher relationships.

How the right relationships are built within the school is naturally something that needs to be discussed in detail, as they are vital to the extended external relationships.

Obviously, this development of close links and relationships with parents by teachers (and please note throughout that the stress is 'with teachers', not just the head teacher) would be fundamentally a bad thing if the aims and aspirations of parents and teachers were diametrically opposed. This is indeed the territory where the sociologist seems sometimes anxious to do battle. But how rarely within my experience is this truly the case. This fact is also borne out by the highly significant answers given in the National Survey found in Volume 2 of the Plowden Report, where all social classes were investigated. Parents of all kinds, classes and groups are genuinely concerned about their children and their futures. The perennial cry is 'I want them to have a better deal than we had!' This is to my mind a good, positive statement on which the discerning teacher can build. The thing to ensure is that the teacher has the freedom, facilities and abilities necessary to communicate and discuss constructively with parents. In order to move forward from this common ground of seeing that John and Mary have a 'better deal' it is a basic necessity for the teacher to know the common ground. For the teacher who ignorantly or unconcernedly sets up a system of clashing values and standards has thereby immediately created divisions, animosities and frustrations.

We must acknowledge that it is the teacher who has all the natural advantages in the situation, and it is he or she who must be the prime mover. The approaches made by the teacher must be varied and continuous and, above all, he must be prepared for either initial rebuff, seeming hostility or criticism perhaps, or certainly no burning enthusiasm in the early stages from the majority of parents. Odd as it may seem, all this does not contradict my previous statements but, as will be explained later, is a traditional defence posture which arises invariably from memories of their own school days.

Dr Johnson remarked of friendship that 'it must be kept in constant repair.' I think communication of this kind must also be kept in constant repair. But once the initial 'priming of the pump' has been undertaken by the teacher it then becomes a real 'two stroke engine'. It is this move forward which leads to the desired educational, sociological and psychological advantages with which we are ultimately concerned.

Imp to mention on attitudes. + even how to actually START bridging gap.

Chapter 2

[handwritten: Social class & parental involve...]

Parents' views and attitudes: a balance sheet

[handwritten: books.]

It is now possible for teachers to investigate a whole range of research findings on the views and attitudes of parents. This reading should strengthen their resolve to develop parent-teacher relationships when they have digested the facts and conclusions contained in these researches. The works of Michael Young and Patrick McGeeney; Frank Musgrove and Philip H. Taylor; Elizabeth Fraser; J. W. B. Douglas; the National Survey results in Volume 2 of the Plowden Report will all help to shed light and clear up misconceptions. Incidentally, Volume 2 of Plowden is a much under-used and neglected book because it appears to be rather a maze of statistics. I would recommend the reading of Chapter 9 by Roma Morton-Williams in *Family Class and Education,* edited by Maurice Craft, as being an outstanding summary and guide of the statistics for those wishing to explore in depth this particular research.

After this careful appraisal, the conclusions in Musgrove and Taylor's *Society and the Teacher's Role* will be heavily substantiated. They write:

> 'But the area of discrepancy between teachers' aims and what they *imagine* to be parents' is still very large. On the whole, teachers take an unflattering view of parents (and their own aims are remarkably idealistic) seeing them as indifferent to moral training but very concerned with social advancement. In fact, parents were substantially in agreement with teachers. The area of (unnecessary) tension might be considerably reduced if parents and teachers established more effective means of communication.'

[handwritten: DISAGREE]

5

At this stage we will not take up this essential point about communication, but rather make certain that we try to understand both the real concern of parents and the discrepancy in teachers' assessment of this concern.

Apart from the historical and traditional views that parents and teachers have of each other, there is the whole business of 'low expectation' rates. Repeatedly, we find this point emphasised and in particular in the National Survey findings, so that it is clear that neither side expects very much of the other. This is clearly demonstrated, for example, when you consider that the large majority of parents expressed themselves as 'satisfied' with the arrangements for visiting and consultation in their children's schools. How equally satisfying these results must be to the heads of the many schools who have no clearly expressed arrangements for these things! As teachers, we are regularly confronted with the fact that children will live up to, or down to their reputations or classifications. The depressing effects of streaming have been clearly exposed in the primary school, where results show over the period of four years that the 'Cs' became immeasurably more 'C-ish'. And so, in this classification system of parents and teachers, we are brought back to the fact that only when a determined effort is made by teachers and parents to get to know each other really well is it discovered that their aspirations for the children are very much in accord. But if parents and teachers are left in their separate realms their attitudes harden throughout the school experience.

We should remember also, as is clearly written in the Plowden Report,

'Parental attitudes appear as a separate influence because they are not monopolised by any one class. Many manual workers and their wives already encourage their children's efforts to learn. If there are many now, there can be even more later. Schools can exercise their influence not only directly upon children, but also indirectly through their relationships with parents.'

There is so much of value and practical guidance in the Plowden Report that it is sad that for many, this may now become just another in a line of reports and an historical document. There is also much that needs to be looked at in a positive and almost 'treasure-seeking' way in order to find the 'clue lines' that will lead to a real breakthrough and growth in parent-teacher understanding. A good example of this is to be found in the analysis of the views of parents on their visits to schools. Tucked away among the low expectancy rate and complacency figure is the comment 'Almost a third [of parents] thought the teacher should have asked them more about their children'.

What a revelation of two attitudes that were sincerely held! On the teachers' side we will be charitable and assume that this disinclination to allow the parent to talk more arose, not from the teachers' verbosity or garrulity, but rather from their wish not to 'quiz' the parent too deeply. Yet here we have a clearly expressed parents' attitude which shows concern and a desire to help that is not being reciprocated by the teacher. This, I believe, proves again how vital it is that all teachers should have some training in the technique of interview or conference sessions with parents.

Another good point arising from the National Survey results which has to be 'gleaned' and thought through is the consideration of the views and attitudes of parents towards homework. Again, it is so easy to classify this in terms of opposing attitudes of teachers and parents. The Survey revealed that the large majority of all parents would like homework to be given to their children. The retort from schools has so often been 'We are debarred from setting homework by the rules of the local education authority' or, more crudely, 'All the parents want is for us to coach their children for the 11 + *and* land ourselves with a lot of extra marking!'. Yet how many others have found that by meeting this request (and thus building a relationship of acceptance rather than rejection) they have further brought home and school closer together.

• Homework does not have to be exclusively computational arithmetic or grammatical exercises, but can also easily be some researching and recording in the immediate environment of the home and district; a practical investigation exercise within the home which will bring parent and child together on the production of a piece of work or even the watching of a TV programme together. This has been strikingly proved to me in two different schools where, in an attempt to assist parents in coping with the long summer holidays (itself a problem often ignored by teachers), we arranged for a whole range of holiday competitions for the children. Nearly all these could enlist the aid of adults since they took the form of observing, collecting and recording in various ways, and all of them could be undertaken in the immediate area of home and school or when away on trips. This, by our definition, was home-work—work to be done away from the classroom and in the home. The competitions resulted, first, in good exhibitions after the long holiday, from which came a great deal of follow-up work within the school, and second in the linking of home and school activities in a real and worthwhile way.

Here then is an opportunity that many teachers have spurned out of hand because of their imagined difference in attitude between parents and teachers over the whole concept of homework.

Primary teachers who are working with their classes along lines so different from the traditional classroom of the thirties and forties (sometimes the kind of classroom parents were taught in) are often the ones who start by having difficulties with parents. Unless real and patient understanding is shown these difficulties can harden into inflexible attitudes, which is a tragic situation from many angles. The teacher who meets repeatedly the question about 'multiplication tables', 'spellings', marks and positions in class etc., so often gets into a very defensive position which results in a feeling of mutual dissatisfaction between the articulate teacher and the apparently inarticulate parents. It is necessary to write 'apparently inarticulate' because, as we shall discuss later, when thinking about the problem of communication, this is largely a linguistics matter, and in fact, with patience and skill, any teacher can deal successfully with these parents' questions. It must always be remembered that the vast majority of parents have a concern and regard for their children, but need help in understanding the stages and factors in the growth and development of human beings. At the end of the day, parents will respect and accept the changes in a school's working pattern and aims once they are convinced that the teachers 'know what they are about' and have a real concern and care for their children.

With the boys and girls in a class it is vital that the teacher begins his work from 'where the child is' and not half way along a new road. Similarly, with parents, no generous assumptions should be made of how much is understood about the contemporary school and its working patterns and organisation. In most of the parents' minds are memories of regimentation, marks (in books and on hands) and a formal subject timetable. But no amount of lectures or written handouts will produce sympathetic understanding of what the school is about. The only real thing that will convince parents of the soundness and worth-whileness of the school and its teachers' work is the regular opportunity to talk with the teacher and see the school at work. The normal hardworking teacher will then by his witness convince the parents that (a) as a professional he knows what he is about and (b) he knows his children and cares about their growth and development.

As Musgrove and Taylor have shown, when this dialogue takes place it is surprising how little discrepancy there really is between the aims and attitudes of parents and teachers, and this applies to all socio-economic classes.

In attempting to draw up a balance sheet of the gains and losses incurred by a school and staff who work at a programme of home and school co-operation and involvement, it is necessary to think, in this order, of the teacher, the child, the parent, the school and the community.

· I deliberately put the teacher first since under any system of public institutionalised education the teacher must be the key figure. Hysterical critics of the home and school movement appear to think that we advocates discount entirely the need and value of the professional in the school situation. They imagine we would settle perhaps for a kind of aircraft hangar peopled only by children and a conveyor belt of any adult who can be cajoled to mind, entertain or enlighten the completely 'free' children wishing to explore their world!

But in the real situation the teacher's gains would be: the gathering of extra knowledge about the child which would help him both to understand him and better plan his work programme; the freedom from much of the stress of discipline problems, since discipline would be a concern really shared with the parents; practical assistance both in the classroom and out of it, on expeditions for example; and the extra interest and perspective which all these factors would add to his job.

On the debit side, he would need to put in some additional hours actually in the school building—but not necessarily *extra* hours, since teachers already work at home.

The teacher would lose some sense of power or omnipotence, since he would no longer be the sole agent in the child's learning programme. This *could* be offset by the enhanced feeling of professional competence that comes from seeing the genuine admiration parents have for the teacher's skill and patience and of the organising role he plays when he has a group of aides working with him in the classroom.

What does the child gain? School becomes a shared experience with his parents and the child *knows* that his parents have both knowledge and understanding of this part of his world. How often in the 'normal' situation does a parent get a rebuff, or the infuriating answer 'Nothing', when he asks 'What have you done in school today?' This response is given because the child knows that to attempt to explain would involve him in a long description which is just beyond him in scope or energy. In a real partnership situation the stress and strain of school is removed and work and expeditions are tackled as exciting or interesting joint ventures. With many children, the warm, satisfying feeling of 'My teacher and mum and dad are friends' leads to greater effort and attainment. It does *not* mean in the correct set-up that a child has to share *everything*, losing all feeling or desire for independence. Just as in even the open plan school there is a quiet room or withdrawal room, so are children allowed and encouraged to work privately and individually on many occasions.

It is difficult to know what to put on the debit side for the child, since obviously the problem of the child whose parents do not co-operate or get involved is in the minority and should not be included in this assessment. Also the 'isolate' is a problem and the teacher needs more than the parent to help him deal with such a child, as indeed the parent needs more than the teacher's assistance.

After twenty-five years' experience and reading a great deal of others' experience, it is difficult for me to point to losses for the child. Some few children seem initially not to want their parents in school. For them, the answer always is to see that their parents *do* come, but that they work in other parts of the school. When it is the norm for parents to be in school, these objectors diminish and their worries about the situation disappear.

What do parents gain? First, and most important, greater under-standing and knowledge of their own children, plus real evidence of their ability to help their children whatever their own education has been. Second, an additional interest in life which is linked with their family. The various clubs and practical activities which a school can provide are limitless and, particularly on a new estate, can mean the end of isolation and neurosis.

On the other hand, all of these things use up time and if parents say they just do not have the time, no moralising or lecturing will alter things. Their priorities are wrong, but only after observing and learning from their peers and neighbours will change take place. So often the relationship is still-born because teachers *will* lecture and *seem* to tell parents how to do their job.

The gains for a school are found mainly in the totally different atmosphere of an open school. The school is no longer an island. Movement in and out of the school is purposeful and proud, and there is a feeling of belonging among everyone concerned which permeates every corner and every person. Helpers abound, problems are shared, and solutions found that just would not occur in the closed school.

On the other hand, teachers have to be accepted as persons and removed from pedestals of either isolation or veneration. In an open situation, it is impossible for anyone to put on an act permanently. Therefore, in the end, everyone—teacher, parent and child acts and talks more naturally, since the situation is more natural. I think the best comparison to make is one with the kind of talk which used to go on in a formal classroom of a closed school. This consisted, more often than not, of a stilted dialogue between a class teacher and thirty or forty children with the real talk carried on behind books or hands. Should a parent or visitor appear, a deathly hush settled, followed after a time by uproar, depending on the duration of the stay and the toughness of the discipline or sanctions within the school.

From the community's viewpoint on the gains made by this kind of parent-teacher partnership, we now have a great deal of additional evidence from Professor Halsey's *Report on the Educational Priority Areas and Projects,* and the lessons to be learned from the report are applicable to all involved in education. Dr Eric Midwinter, addressing the British Association at its 1971 meeting said,

> 'The legend of working class parental lethargy must be abandoned. A community school in an inner city zone could do more than enlist the help of parents who would like their children to break out of the vicious circle of poor living conditions and expectations. It could aim to revitalise a "rundown" community or rejuvenate one which was redeveloped or transported to a new housing estate. Such a school could have a strong emphasis upon environmental studies and skills.'

It would seem, therefore, that the gains are overwhelmingly in favour of developing a partnership community school at all levels and in all situations.

Chapter 3

Where do we begin?

How do we bridge the gap?
- t's still make 1st move.

Having considered why we need to understand and work with parents and having also assessed both parents' attitudes and the gains and losses of such a changed pattern of relationships, inside and outside the school, how then do we begin and what will be the stages of development?

In chapter 1 I emphasised that it is the teacher who has all the natural advantages in the situation and that he or she should be the prime mover. Any head, teacher or school who argued 'Well, we are quite willing to develop relations and co-operation with parents, but we are waiting for the parents to request this', will probably have to wait a very long while. This stems back to the 'low expectancy' rates of parents based largely upon the memories of their own school days. Nevertheless, in talking to parents in many parts of England, I have often been asked, 'How do parents go about obtaining an open school situation or even the setting up of a PTA if the school gives no lead?' The answer given to this question can only be very limited and general, since each local situation will have different elements within it. It is necessary to stress that the head and staff are the professionals and that the head must still, at the time of writing, under the articles of government 'control the internal organisation, management and discipline of the school'. These responsibilities are carried out within the context of what the articles refer to as the governors'/managers' 'general direction of the conduct and curriculum of the school'. It would seem, therefore, that with the welcome widening of the recruitment of school managers and governors to include parents of the school, such matters as parental involvement and co-operation within the school situation may well be discussed at managers' and governors' meetings in future, when recommendations can be made.

I have always urged such parents raising the question of PTAs to try a less 'political' approach in the first instance. It would seem that if a group of parents who are keen to 'open up' the school go individually to the head and volunteer their services *in any capacity* it will be a very shortsighted head who refuses another pair of hands! I have always stressed that numbers involved in the early stages are unimportant, that the kinds of task are immaterial and that it is the establishing of the principle that counts. Once teachers and parents are talking and working together—alongside each other for the common benefit of the school and its children—then, given normal good fortune, the situation will grow and develop naturally.

In considering the question from the school's side, however, it is necessary to examine the many different starting points and also the variations within these depending on how far head and staff agree or disagree upon the whole question.

In very broad terms, I would suggest that there are four different kinds of school situation in the context of parent–teacher relations.

First of all, and still in existence, despite the legendary quality they have now acquired, there are what I call the old 'Keep Out' notice schools. It is still possible to find many schools exhibiting notices which have a definite deterrent effect on parents wishing to go into the school. Some are rather thoughtlessly worded; some are put up with good intentions, such as the very large and all-dominating notice which says No Parents' Cars Beyond This Point. It is obvious to all that *other* cars can go in, but *not* parents' cars! It can be argued that everyone understands that this is a road safety measure, but I maintain that it merely reinforces in many parents' minds an idea that school is not for them. I believe a more telling prominent notice could have read Parents Welcome, But Not Their Cars, Beyond This Point, Please!

In a similar vein, I think the notices found in many schools which say All Parents Must See (or even *report* to!) the Head or Secretary before Entering the School or Appointments to See the Head must be Made in Advance through the Secretary, and variations on these two themes, all tend to discourage rather than encourage parents.

Of course, such notices can be defended, but all I am arguing is that if we genuinely want to open our schools, then we must make real efforts to see that they are welcoming, easy and comfortable places to enter.

The Welsh, and many others, have a very felicitous habit of putting up welcome signs to their country and their towns and villages; how good it would be to see similar notices outside all our schools!

The second category of school is what I term the neutral school. It is a school which has removed its offending notices, but has made no other gestures of real welcome to its parents. Without notices, it quietly but firmly creates the atmosphere inside and out which says to parents 'We work *inside* here and your job is to support us *outside* the school'. This is very often a laudable school situation (in all but this one vital respect) with teachers working hard and conscientiously. However, because the parents are kept outside the school and have the minimum of communication, the staff have, unnecessarily, to put up with too many discipline problems and too many under-achieving children. To the staff, however, there is nothing unusual in their situation (and, to be fair, theirs is not the unusual situation, for around 60 per cent of schools have similar conditions).

It is within the neutral schools that in the end could come the greatest breakthrough and happily there are some signs of this occurring. The interesting and encouraging thing here is that the breakthrough often comes from the individual class teacher and *not* as a result of the head's policy. The explanation of this will be found after we have considered the next two categories of school.

The third category of school I label as the PTA school, and in many ways this presents, surprisingly, the saddest of the school situations. At some stage or other in the school's story it was decided (more often than not by an arbitrary act of the head's) to have a parent-teacher association. Such associations have existed in some schools for many years and some go back to pre-World War Two, but the real growth came in the 1950s and early 1960s. To keep this in perspective, however, let it be noted that they still had not reached more than 17 per cent. of the schools by the time of the Plowden Report's publication. For a variety of reasons schools formed PTAs, but, whatever the reasons (and I believe most had genuine and not band-wagon motives), their development has followed along almost stereotyped lines. They had constitutions, and the only clause that mattered was 'The headmaster's decision is final' and more often than not it added that the chairman *must* be head of the school! In terms of activities the pattern was almost exclusively one of money-raising; head's talks or lectures; occasional films or visiting speakers or some social activity (linked with money-raising). The attendances were predictable and the absentees equally predictable. Before I am accused of sounding both belittling and sneering, let me state that I formed three such PTAs myself in my first three headships.

What I now feel, and I am delighted that the General Secretary of the National Confederation of PTAs, John Hale, has publicly said in effect the same thing, is that the anglicised version of the PTA is not necessarily the only way to develop good parental involvement and co-operation within the school situation. What Dr Douglas, Patrick McGeeney, Michael Young and the Plowden Report have shown are the good effects on children, their work and development, when parents are interested *and* involved in the school's work programme and with its teachers. Many of the normal PTAs activities do not achieve this involvement, nor embrace enough of the parents.

For some time I was head of an international primary school, with over 80 per cent of its children American, and it was there that I learned what is meant by real parental involvement. Once it was known that I was a believer in PTAs the offers of help flooded in from the mothers and fathers. To me and my largely British staff, this was incredible. Parent–teacher association to these American parents meant giving of time and effort to the school. It meant a willingness to do yard (playground) duty, accompanying children on trips, working on stock and in the library, helping to wash dishes and pots and even offering to do the school garden. And what of the desire to 'rule the school', to usurp the teacher's function? Of course, these parents wanted to know about our work programme and they questioned what we were doing. As a result of this, many would argue and discuss the pros and cons of what we were doing, but, and this is the truly significant thing that struck us all so forcibly, at the end of the day they would concede, 'Well, you're the professional. Go ahead—let's see how it works!' This neatly and graciously put us in the role of the true professional with the expertise. In other words, far from diminishing our role as teachers, the PTA (American) set-up enhanced our position.

Strengthened by these experiences, I returned to England and learned of course that what I had experienced had also been learned now by pioneers like Jack Solomons in Cornwall, Charles Betty in Kent, Harry Stephenson in London and many others. I did not, therefore, form a PTA in my next school, but the staff and I jointly worked at securing real involvement and partnership with our parents. After some four years in a non-middle class area, it was recognised by many visitors that we had achieved a great deal and much more than many felt possible in such socio-economic circumstances.

Briefly, my fourth category of school is the true community school and as yet not many are to be found. Here, there is the really open situation where communication, involvement, assistance, joint activities and concern are found between all sections of the community, embracing the young, middle-aged and elderly. The school building itself may well contain even the local branch of the county library, a coffee bar and community workshops. The work of men like Cyril Poster and Edward Walls makes valuable and encouraging reading, and not least because here we have the work patterns and relationships extended to the secondary level and not just to the primary schools. While it is a natural development, in one sense, for the teenager to grow away from the family, it has not been found either in England, Scandinavia, Russia or America that more difficulties are caused (rather the reverse) by parents continuing to take an interest and active part in their children's education and school programmes.

How can bridge be gapped - how do you start?

In whatever category of school teachers may be working, it is obviously possible to start or extend their work with parents. The main question here is, does this have to start with head and staff together resolved, or can a start be made by a head in isolation or a class teacher in isolation?

Providing there have been good preparatory discussions and an understanding of why the school should now become open and extend its direct contact with parents, it is naturally better for the head and staff to work together. But, equally, either party can 'go it alone', with again the same proviso about knowing why you are about this business and also, equally important, what you are about with John and Mary.

Once a school is determined to work at home and school relationships, everything that has gone before must be closely scrutinised and evaluated. Everything, that is, which affects the parents in their contact with the school, its building and its teachers and ancillary workers.

The criterion must be, is the school an easy, welcoming and comfortable place to enter? I have seen educational priority schools of the three-decker variety transformed from grim, penitentiary buildings into colourful and comfortable places without enormous sums of money being spent. The building need not be a bar to a start being made.

Conversely, I have seen a few brand new buildings which are so clinically correct, yet have no outward and visible signs that a parent could just pop in, browse or sit. So it is quite wrong to generalise about age or architectural fashion being a necessary ingredient. (The same remark could in its way apply equally to teachers!)

The forbidding or negative notices having been removed, substitution of some positive and welcoming notices and displays must rank among the first priorities. The provision of a parents' room is not yet conceded in new school design. Many older schools have still only recently acquired worthwhile staff rooms, therefore numbers of us must settle for only a special parents' notice board, and book or work displays aimed at parents in the entrance or corridors. These are not frills though, and they do help to convey the message of 'Welcome! This is our school—what more can you do to help?'

1st thing

Heads and teachers need to be seen more easily as approachable in an informal way, and this is particularly so at the beginning or end of sessions. Of course, the children come first and parents will both expect and understand this. They are not convinced, and neither am I, that a head needs to be buried in his room feverishly engaged upon administrative matters at the beginning and end of every school session! Neither are parents, or any heads, convinced that teachers should be seen rushing off to catch buses or trains at 4.15 p.m. each day. What other worker clocks in at 9 a.m. and is out at 4.15 p.m.? And to those who say 'But what other worker has two or three hours' work to do in the evening?' the effective answer is 'Try to do this work at school'. Your stock will rise with head and parents and, what is more, all you

15

need for the job should be to hand! The main thing, however, is to convince parents that you are available and easily approachable. In the early days of a campaign to achieve partnership I would recommend that the school should be open regularly once a month in the evening. This should be a really informal free time for any parents just to come in to look round, examine work, books or apparatus or talk with the head or any of the teachers, and is completely different from the formal set-up conference sessions to be discussed in chapter 6. Some parents will merely come in and talk with each other, and in new estate areas this provides a most valuable experience. To critics who say that this stretches our social work too far and that our concern is education, a reminder is necessary that John and Mary are more likely to settle and grow if Mum and Dad are contented, than if there is strain and unsettled conditions at home.

In Patrick McGeeney's books and in Volume 1 of the Plowden Report, many excellent examples are given of opportunities provided by schools to involve and draw in their parents. As with written communication, no one way is guaranteed, and as many different activities as possible should be provided, since some will appeal to one parent but not to another.

Attendance at school assemblies, coffee mornings on a class basis, joint children-parent lunchtime concerts in aid of some current good cause all not only bring parents into the school, but provide worthwhile and real opportunities for children's work and social development.

Small discussion groups one evening a month (numbers are not important) reach another segment of the school's parents. From groups like these, held over two years in my last school, five mothers sought enrolment on a mature students teacher training course.

Completely informal sessions where parents can use children's art and craft materials and explore reading or mathematical structural apparatus all lead to more worthwhile exchanges than a dozen lectures or talks by head or staff.

Invitations to come in and form working parties during school time (and for some fathers in the evening) to repair or make apparatus give the lead in to other very necessary chores that many of us have found parents will gladly, gratefully and happily do once they are really accepted as partners in the education of their children. For the first few weeks it is a good idea to have a list of jobs on display which parents can choose from. If included among the last are some requiring the minimum of intellectual effort, whilst others are perhaps more in the line of cataloguing or sorting, the word soon spreads round that there is something for everyone, and the diffident venture forth. But, once again, numbers are not important. Three or four parents only will noise it abroad (and so will the children) and the numbers are soon so large that teachers begin to wonder how they ever managed without parents!

Some schools develop purely social events, such as organised theatre trips and beauty and fashion displays. Here it nearly always seems to be that a member of the staff or a parent has really found a niche as entertainments organiser, and provided that a genuine need is being met only good can come of this piece of community work.

The question now is: how far can or should a teacher go in isolation? In the extreme case, a head could make it virtually impossible for a teacher to develop personal contacts with the parents of the children in his class. If such an attitude were adopted by the head, then the teacher would probably be better off in every way by leaving the school and seeking a new post. Since strong official approval has now been given by the Department of Education and Science for the development of good home and school links, the teacher would in no way suffer professionally by the move.

Where a teacher is made to feel very conscious of a staff's hostility to any attempts he or she may be making to establish contacts with the parents of her class, I would suggest a decision as to whether or not he or she should remain would depend very much on the head's support and wishes.

What are the things a teacher can do in isolation on a staff? During the last three years, while working in a college of education, I have been tremendously encouraged to discover how much our students can do. I have also seen several instances where because of what one teacher has achieved, others have slowly followed suit.

First and foremost, a great deal can be started by being around at moments when parents are at the door or at the gates. If shopping can be done locally, then by just meeting parents in the supermarket it will be seen that you are friendly and approachable. If the teacher can join in various community activities, either sporting or recreational, again the gap is narrowed, the pedestal removed or the bridge constructed.

Short notes written home with queries or questions about the children or requests that Mum and Dad might drop in to discuss a definite point are again within the range and ability of most teachers. How often a teacher will be invited into homes or seek invitations is very much a personal matter. Where it can be done easily and naturally only good can be the result.

Almost any of the previous suggestions for activities can be modified and scaled down for the class teacher, and it is when these are successfully attempted that a breakthrough really begins.

As with so much else in life, it is the first faltering and diffident moves that are the most difficult, but truly in this sphere nothing succeeds like success. Careful and thorough preparation is necessary once it is clear why partnership with parents is being sought. The following chapters deal with the problems of written and spoken communication; again much of what follows is applicable for either the head and staff working together or for the class teacher as a 'loner'.

Chapter 4

Using the printed word

If there is one central message in connection with the establishment of right relationships between home and school it is, paradoxically, that there is no one way or method. It will be in the multiplicity of contacts, communications and approaches that success will be found. But having stated that, a beginning must nevertheless be made somewhere.

I am a great believer in starting with the school prospectus. The Plowden Report recommended specifically that schools should prepare a booklet giving parents the basic facts about the school and its organisation, internally and externally, and how to get and keep in touch with teachers. By setting yourself the task of writing such a booklet you have to crystallise your own thoughts on the kind of school image you are attempting to create in the eyes of the community. When writing this you are obliged to go through the priorities of school living, working and growing. Any good school will continue to change and develop over the years and it is not recommended that an elaborate, glossy and 'once for all' production is necessary. An attractive cover is essential in these days of high standards of presentation in advertising, and therefore the help of the graphics department of the nearest school of art should be sought. But the inserts should be duplicated sheets of information which can be frequently revised.

An outlined prospectus for a primary school is included in the appendix and from this you will see that one message is repeated in several different ways. Parents are invited freely and informally into school for a variety of reasons: to get to know the class teacher; to see what TV programmes are being used and how; to see holiday dates on the parents' notice board; to join in assemblies; to join workshops, social events, trips, or even to wash up paint pots.

The prospectus is useful for new parents coming from other education authorities and also for those coming from a neighbouring school. To assume that because parents live locally they have a reasonable amount of information is quite erroneous. Most teachers are aware of the distortions which exist about the activities of particular schools. These 'legends' reinforce the need for a clear statement of a school's intention and an open school policy so that all may freely come to see what is really happening.

It has been apparent to many, long before John Holt's admirable books *How Children Fail* and *How Children Learn,* that so often what we say and what we write is not understood by either children or parents. This is not because of lack of intelligence or lack of desire to know, but purely because of language difficulties. It is absolutely essential that we write clear and simple English in a style acceptable and understood by parents. A study of the national press and a vocabulary count and sentence structure analysis of, say the *Guardian* and *The Daily Mirror* would be an instructive exercise for many heads.

After the prospectus, I think much more consideration should be given to the notes or letters which the school sends home. Every school sends letters to parents to announce school functions, changes in school organisation, rules and regulations, closures, etc. From these irregular and varied letters a more planned type of letter with wide coverage can evolve. I am suggesting that every school should consider sending home a termly or monthly newsletter. If it is known that at regular intervals these letters will be sent home, then quite often by careful anticipation all announcements can be included in the appropriate issue. Occasionally, of course, an ordinary letter will still be necessary for the unexpected and emergency announcement.

Where the newsletter is adopted and becomes an integral part of the school scene, each issue should be numbered. This numbering is quite an important small fact since it helps both to stress a continuity and develop a tradition. Anniversaries are important within a school, a family and a community and 'Our 10th Edition' may somehow make a few more parents decide to read on rather than consign it to the dustbin or the back shelf of the bureau.

Into the newsletter will go not just the announcements already mentioned but also brief 'plugs' regarding policies and philosophies behind the working pattern of the school. These messages over a period of time can be absolutely invaluable in creating both the right ethos and relationships.

Allied to this I also recommend the production of a parent-staff magazine or just a parents' magazine. Should this seem completely impractical then some of the items I suggest for this could equally well go into an extended newsletter. However, I do believe from experience and observation in several schools that a parents' magazine can be an exceptionally helpful piece of work for binding home and school together. This is not so 'way out' as you would imagine and certainly should not be taken as only suitable for middle class or suburban areas. I have seen very creditable and valuable magazines produced in what are undoubtedly deprived areas socially and culturally.

Into these pages will go school family news, not just about boys and girls and staff, but events that have happened to any who work in the school or visit it from the immediate neighbourhood. These are the threads that help to join together school and community. In an overspill area where I once worked, parents commented that these small items, which would not have reached the professional press, have both interested them and given them a feeling of belonging.

It is in these pages also that some will write up their queries and express their puzzlement at various happenings. Critical articles must be included, since these will give piquancy to the dish, and will often also evoke from others good, constructive and highly original replies. These accounts of things seen and heard in the school will be that much more effective because they are written by parents.

Reviews of children's books and suggestions for Christmas and birthdays are another valuable contribution and are much appreciated by all members of the family. Here the co-operation of an interested and understanding local librarian can be sought.

Advertisements of the *Exchange & Mart* kind will not only perform a useful service to parents (especially where there is a school uniform in existence) but will help to make the whole publication commercially viable.

In England, the local paper is a tradition and so it is wrong in these days of the massive appeal of TV to disparage the printed word. Marshall McLuhan may well be right in his final analysis regarding the eventual disappearance of this medium, but at present the printed news from around the parish pump is still one of our best methods of communication.

It follows naturally, therefore, that any school wishing to link home, school and community will not only always be alert for other opportunities to disseminate information to parents but will have material available and at the ready. From so many angles, it is a wise move to get to know the editor of the local paper; the vicar and all ministers of religion in the area; community, consumers' and residents' association officers. All or any of these will, in lean times for 'copy', ask if you have anything for them. Short articles on aims and objectives in education or accounts of interesting and original pieces of work or research that have taken place in the school will then be very welcome and will have added to the understanding, knowledge and sympathy regarding the school's work within the community.

The development of local radio offers a wonderful opportunity to reach another group of adults. The possibilities here, judging from what happens in America and Australia, are almost limitless. But be very much on your guard that your contributions are not used in any competitive way so that it appears that X primary school is always seeking publicity. Instead, most of the contributions should be seen as furthering the cause of education generally, rather than the merits of one school as compared with another.

Finally in this section, which is mainly concerned with making contacts through the written word, we can consider the one sheet of information which has always gone home to the parents—whatever category of school is concerned: the school report. Recently, there have been some very interesting contributions on the subject of school reports from the Home and School Council (*Information for Parents*) and from the Advisory Centre for Education, Cambridge. To sum up the new directions in which these are being developed one can do no better than to use Laurence Green's phrase and refer to the need for the 'two-way report'. A development of his ideas and many other useful suggestions will be found in his book *Parents and Teachers: Partners or Rivals?*

Many of us through the years have discovered that added notice, value and interest is forthcoming if the parents have to contribute more than their signature after a cursory reading. I write 'cursory reading' since so many reports receive, and deserve, only that. If the stereotyped 'good', 'fair', 'could do better' report is sent home with the emphasis upon little boxes with their marks, letter gradings or positions inscribed therein, then productive communication between teacher and taught, parent and teacher, cannot grow.

If, on the other hand, the report is written so that it becomes a personal account of each child's development and contains suggestions and questions, it will elicit response from and involvement by the parent. Obviously this kind of report takes longer to compile, although this can be disputed if within the school a running 'profile' is kept for each child throughout the year. It is, however, a productive, open-ended document, for the parents are invited to reply on the back of the report. I found, and many others have also, that a great deal of helpful information flowed in from these two-way reports and follow-up talks with parents became a natural corollary. For primary school children I would go as far as to suggest that the report does become identical to a letter (for one thing, a letter so often presupposes a reply) and that the only structure it takes would be in the paragraphing of the contents in a form approximately identical for all children.

Where the staff decide to use all of these means of communication to the full, one can almost guarantee improved relationships and certainly many fewer problems and crises within the school situation.

Chapter 5

Problem of communication

Everyone concerned with the training of teachers has a pet ingredient which they feel 'must' be included in the course. Obviously if all of these had to be fitted in, a teacher's working life might well be halved, for it would be a truly formidable total of training time required! For me it is a source of amazement that so many young teachers arrive in school without having had any opportunity to study in some depth the varied problems of language, talking and communication. We say we are well out of the 'chalk and talk' era and we applaud that fact. The interesting thing to me, however, is that teachers in the informal, flexible, working alongside-the-child situation are actually talking much more than they ever did before! But investigate how far they have considered the whole question of linguistics; what they know of the speech concept of 'register'; how far they consider this quotation from an excellent chapter by Denis Lawton in *Family, Class and Education*: 'The Bernstein theory provides us with a much superior springboard for action than vaguer notions of culture clash or poor motivation.' The poor results of such enquiries among young teachers are sad because it means so often that they too, despite all kinds of good intentions, often join the numbers of teachers who flood their children with a deluge of incomprehensible sounds.

The difficulties of communication between children and teachers because of the differing speech codes often apply equally to the communication difficulties between teacher and parents. It is interesting that Dr Lawton concludes that because of speech differences the characteristics displayed (by the speaker) will often be interpreted by teachers 'as bad manners, lack of co-operation, poor application to work, poor interest or motivation' whereas in fact it could well be merely a breakdown in effective communication.

Teachers working in what are loosely termed middle-class areas do have other problems of communication, but they are not linguistic ones. The problems for the young teacher particularly in these situations are to have sufficient patience and, whilst being sure of what they are doing, to prevent at all costs a shrill, defensive note creeping into their explanations. In other words, as with everything else in teaching, get to know your children; assess their needs and plan your work programmes to meet these needs. When talking with the parents, therefore, it is from this position of strength that the teacher should seek their assistance *and* advice. 'This is how I see John's needs and this is how we propose dealing with them. Do you see other needs?' If, as is suggested in chapter 6, this discussion about John and his work and growth as a person is being held in a prepared 'conference' session, the teacher will have to hand some evidence of John's needs and the books, materials and apparatus used by him to meet them.

When we come to the business of the teacher in the 'down town' area, or the segregated estate school parents, a whole range of teaching skills and understanding must be brought into play.

I cannot reiterate sufficiently that if the teacher is to develop a worthwhile relationship with any parent, then it must be on a person-to-person basis. If there is even a trace of the clinical or hierarchical role creeping in, it is not likely to grow into a partnership relationship. When we see or hear the Frankie Howerds of today impersonating the curate or vicar, it seems almost unbelievable that such parsonical characters really do still exist. I am forced to believe that they do (even though I have not actually met any) because I still meet nice, good and decent teachers who suddenly put on a clinical, detached kind of voice when discussing John or Mary with Mum and Dad. Hence my plea for naturalness in meeting parents. I think that it is *not* a waste of any teacher's time simply to talk about everyday things for several of their initial meetings with parents. How often have I heard a teacher say in the staff room, 'Well, I'm not paid to talk about the new baby, Mrs. Brown's eldest daughter's wedding, or last night's Morecambe and Wise programme!' The extra sad thing about such statements is that often such teachers could talk very well about those things. If only they would realise that it would not rob them of their professional status, mystique or whatever it is they want to preserve, but in the end might well enhance their image in the eyes of the parent! Parents *know* we are teachers; it is a bonus when they also accept us as pleasant, concerned persons.

Once the person-to-person relationship is established, what a mine of information is then gained about John and Mary! What a difference it makes to the real help a teacher gets from the parents, and how much easier and yet more interesting his work becomes with the children.

It is a truism to write that not all communication is necessarily verbal. Virginia Bailard and Ruth Strang in their fascinating book *Parent-Teacher Conferences* could well overstate their case, but the following two quotations perhaps act as a timely reminder to some:

> 'A teacher may betray a feeling of inferiority by a subdued voice, a sagging posture, downcast eyes, hesitant speech and many other expressive signs. He may express antagonism towards a parent by a brusque manner, a grim facial expression and movements that indicate impatience. One shows genuine regard for another person by giving him close attention, smiling encouragement or approval and considering his physical comfort. The language of behaviour is extensive and subtle. The skilled interviewer is aware of the importance of such non-verbal communication. It is the most effective way of showing a parent that he cares.'

A point which will be stressed again when the question of the formal interview takes place is the need for clarity and the importance of listening in communication.

Bailard and Strang write,

> 'Good communication is clear communication. It will not be clear if each person, because of different background interprets the words differently, or if, as in *Alice in Wonderland,* each person makes a word mean what he chooses it to mean.
>
> 'The more we listen to what the other person wants to tell us, the likelier we are to avoid this danger. If we give him a chance to present himself and his problem in his own way, we gain enough understanding to communicate with him. It is when we begin to be didactic that we lose connection with him.'

Our aim in all of this work is to make connections for the benefit of the children we teach. Faulty communication or non-communication deprives us of these connections.

I would suggest that each young teacher should read through carefully Barnes, Britton and Rosen's book *Language, the Learner and the School.* There is a great deal in this book which will help a teacher to formulate questions, initiate and lead discussions with his children, and much also which will guide him in talking with parents. Some of the taped sequences which are transcribed are so revealing and salutary, and again it is possible to hear echoes of interviews and talks with parents. How utterly infuriating and frustrating it is for an adult to be asked questions which do not really require an answer since the answer is already contained in the question. Or equally, how easy it is not to accept a general answer because it is made abundantly clear by the questioner that the required, specific answer has not yet been forthcoming. As teachers, we are often guilty of these two practices and easily transfer them as a manner of habit to adults with whom we speak. Open-ended discussions are needed.

Alice Yardley, in *Exploration and Language,* highlights both a problem of language and incidentally a problem of training. This observation could well invalidate my claim at the beginning of this chapter, that the study of linguistics and communication should be included in every teacher's training, for it issues a general warning that all of us, as teachers, should heed.

> 'The complexities of becoming familiar with his mother tongue are conquered even by the child with little intelligence. Nearly all forms of human activity will involve him in words, and if he fails to acquire them he fails as a human being. Few people fail in the early stages while learning language is part of living. It is later, when language is sometimes taught as a subject or attempts are made to isolate the study of it, that failure appears.'

As in our written communication with parents, equal care should be taken in our speech. It is important to see that we know what it is we want to say, that it is said with clarity and simplicity (avoiding jargon at all costs) and that having said it we pause and really listen to what the parent may want to say to us. Particularly in the early stages of the relationship, we shall achieve so much more by friendly and intelligent listening than by talking.

Chapter 6

The formal conference

The 'Keep Out' notices are down and 'Welcome' is written large across the school mat. Head and staff have jointly or separately planned a whole series of events and activities which will bring parents into the school. All members of the school family have seized every opportunity both inside school and outside in the community to create links and bridge gaps. Special attention has been given to the many and varied forms of communication, both written and verbal. The whole exercise is well under way and, despite the several rebuffs and failures which are inevitable in this and any other kind of community work, there are encouraging, positive signs that some progress is being made. What then are the practical steps which now need to be undertaken in order to sustain progress, consolidate gains and promote worthwhile developments?

The first thing to do is to see that after the initial enthusiasm and 'Hawthorn effect' of the programme has diminished that the foundations are solid and still intact. If a fixed open night each month has been started, this *must* continue, even though the numbers coming in may well have dropped. The fact is that some parents, long after these early days, will remember this arrangement and while they would not write a note to fix an appointment to see you, they will come along when safe in the knowledge that the school is open and teachers available. Similarly, the parents' notice board must contain lists of jobs and ways in which parents can join in some of the school's programme. There are parents who just could not force themselves to come in and ask what they could do, but, learning of the list, will sidle in and have an oblique look.

But after all of these and similar things have been carried out, the next important thing to organise thoroughly will be the arrangements for parents' interviews, or conferences as the Americans call them. I remember my surprise, in the early days of my headship of the largely American school, being asked, 'And when do you plan on setting up some conferences?'

Following the upsurge of interest in PTAs in the fifties and sixties, many schools started their annual open day. For most, this meant a hectic and hardworking period preparing the most elaborate exhibition of work, and the school having been spring-cleaned, it went en fête. Making a very unnatural corollary to open days, were the long, silent and embarrassed queues of parents at the class teachers' desks. There, in front of everyone, the teacher talked for a few minutes about John and Mary to their respective parents. The result was completely unsatisfactory to the parents and, I suspect, to most teachers. I can recall, however, in some staff rooms the 'one-upmanship' which reigned when brash youngsters would boast 'and I saw fifty-two of my parents in two and a half hours'. And often that was about correct—four minutes a parent! The interesting thing was, and presumably still is in certain schools, that parents continued to come in their droves each year, even though they gained little of value. I think this emphasises very much that parents *are* concerned and will make the effort when opportunities are provided, even when there are very indifferent opportunities. The strange thing that also happened on the teachers' side each year was that afterwards teachers could be heard saying 'Oh, if only I had known that about John *before,* what a difference it would have made'. Yet still, presumably because of the need for a bumper exhibition, the meetings took place at the end of the school year instead of at the beginning.

So what is recommended now in the way of parent-teacher interviews? Definitely, however good the informal meetings are, I still maintain that there is a real need for the prepared conference session between parent and teacher. It has been argued by sociologists that the booked, forward-dated interview is a middle-class idea and that working-class people just do not understand or want it. Maybe at one time they did not, but perhaps the setting up of the welfare state has changed them. All kinds of people are now used to booking ahead for doctors, dentists, garages for car servicing and continental holidays! Certainly it has been the experience of many of us nowadays that a 95 per cent. response from parents for this kind of service is normal. (The odd 5 per cent. will be considered later when the position of teachers/social workers is discussed).

Two conferences with the parents every year form a very reasonable pattern. The first should be in the autumn term, assuming that the school is not vertically or family grouped and that children have been moved into a new class in September. The second conference could well come in the summer term after the parents have received the annual report. The two-way report which was advocated in chapter 4 provides a very good foundation for a follow-up discussion with parents. If, of course, the school is vertically grouped, there is still a need to provide for the formal conference, but it is doubtful whether two would in all cases be necessary each year. The question of home and school relationships within the family grouped school is, of course, in some ways a much easier task, the reason for this being that parents really do get to know their children's teacher in what is a continuous relationship throughout their school lives.

Having decided, therefore, to have the two conferences, it is necessary to consider in some detail their organisational pattern.

A pre-booked and planned-for confrontation of this kind must have as its basic aim the welfare of the boy or girl being discussed. Its aim is not to be a therapy session for the parent or a soft option for the teacher. The parent and teacher sitting down together and discussing the child should achieve an exchange of information and an agreed programme for the future. Greater understanding of the child, and some improved initial understanding of each other by the parent and the teacher should also follow from the discussion. Maybe as a by-product the parent will feel better for having shared some of his worries and thoughts and maybe the teacher's job will have become a little clearer and easier, but these are not the main objectives of this particular exercise.

Knowing in advance which parents are coming for a conference, the teacher will have prepared certain material and also certain questions which he will ask should a suitable opportunity occur. It is more important, however, for the parent to be given plenty of opportunity to ask his or her questions at these sessions, since it is easier for the teacher to *make* other opportunities to ask his if necessary.

The teacher must be quite certain that he has assembled everything he will need in order to talk about John and Mary and develop the points he wants to make. Nothing is more off-putting and distracting than a frantic search through desks, drawers and cupboards during the interview for some book or piece of work. If the need is felt to assert one's professionalism, the quiet efficiency of making one's points with material well to hand is most effective.

The interview will be carried out in privacy and if possible in as comfortable a setting as can be arranged. Bearing in mind that nearly always we want to eradicate parents' memories of their own schooldays, the *last* position to take up is sitting behind a desk with the parent in front of you! Sincere and earnest young teachers have said to me after such face-to-face confrontations 'Oh dear, Mr. Brown was so tense, and I found it such hard going!' I am sure that temporarily Mr Brown had been transported and was once again, in memory, facing his old martinet or dragon of a teacher! As with everything, a swing to the extreme opposite position will be, in its way, equally disastrous and the teacher should not, therefore, drape himself over the chair as if he were about to retire to bed!

On entering the room and being greeted by the teacher, the parent should be offered a chair at the teacher's side. This is not a moment to begin with a light-hearted conversational gambit about the weather or the Test match. This is a conference about John or Mary. Nevertheless, your opening remark could well be a sincerely meant appreciation of the parent's giving up some of his time to visit the school.

Next, if it is at all possible, continue with an honest, positive statement about the child concerned. Maybe the parent will interrupt with some down to earth remark about John's lack of effort or attainment, or about his behaviour, and whilst this (like any other contribution from the parent) must *not* be brushed aside, try to return to your *good, positive* statement. Genuinely you are on the child's side and most parents will warm to the teacher if he makes it plain that he cannot be shifted from that position. This does not imply that the teacher is *against* the parent. One thing I learned the hard way in my dealings with parents is that very often the parent who complains the most about his or her child is the one who loves and cares the most. Do not fall into the trap of agreeing that Mary really is a little so-and-so, or you will nearly always alienate yourself from the parent.

If a parent persists in listing complaints about the child, move in with your questions. 'Why do you think John acts like that? How long has John been like this, and how did it all start?'

Avoid at all costs launching into a lecture and certainly never dogmatise on how parents should rear their children.

As I have said, the aims of the conference are to make the parent aware that you care for children's growth and development and that you need the parent's help and support in order to further these during the coming school year. But if the whole idea of this help is left in vague terms the conference will end with an unsatisfied feeling on the parent's side. What are needed are some practical suggestions by the teacher of ways in which parent and child can work or play together which will stimulate the child's intellectual or social growth. There will be points which the teacher will already have prepared, and some of these will be common to all parents (and do not forget that parents, as well as teachers, swap tales!) and some will be tailored for that particular child. It is equally important for the parent to leave realising it was not just a once and for all time visit. Try to get the parent to agree on a further visit which will take place in school time. This further visit can well be connected with the jobs listed on the parents' notice board or with your suggestions regarding their joint work or play activities with their child.

In general terms I believe it is vital for the success of the conferences that we teachers accept the following propositions as laid down by Bailard and Strang:

1 Parents, like all other people, need acceptance and approval. Blaming the parents gets us nowhere.
2 Parents want honest, up-to-date, accurate information and not platitudes and vague generalisations.
3 Parents are often both relieved and helped by hearing how other parents have handled problems similar to their own.

Hefferman and Todd in *The Elementary Teacher's Guide to Working with Parents* give the following as their aims for parent conferences:

1 To enable the home and the school to meet the needs of the child most effectively.
2 To establish a working relationship with parents in the interest of the child.
3 To assure a two-way communication between home and school.
4 To share with parents what is known about the growth characteristics and needs of specific age groups.
5 To share with the parents the educational programme which has been based on these growth characteristics and designed to meet the needs of the children.
6 To help parents understand the role of education in a democratic society.
7 To suggest ways parents can help children succeed in school.
8 To arrive at common objectives for home and school.
9 To interpret to parents their child's growth and progress in his school work.
10 To share with parents professional knowledge about social and emotional developments of children.
11 To help teachers acquire understanding of the child's relationships to his parents, brothers and sisters, and other family members.
12 To help the teacher understand the family aspirations for the child, his rarities, interests, out-of-school activities, and the emotional tone of his home.
13 To provide opportunities for the teacher to perceive the parents' reaction to the school.
14 To help parents recognise the individual parent-teacher conference as an indispensable part of a modern education programme.

Naturally, many will see this list as too ambitious for our present scale of achievement, but if only some of these aims are abstracted and accepted, further practical organisational steps will have to be considered within the school.

If my original suggestion, that there should be two conferences a year, is accepted, at what time of day should they be held and for what numbers should they be planned?

Where a school is fortunate in having a flexible timetable and a head who works alongside his teachers, and perhaps a few part-time staff, some appointments for the conferences could be arranged during the daytime school session. Most schools, however, settle for having them all in the evenings. In any case, most fathers need to have them after their working hours. Suitable accommodation must also be available and this again restricts the times for some schools. As a rough guide, if two hours is set aside in the evening, no more than five conferences should be booked in and a teacher can roughly assume that two and a half hours is in fact more likely to be used up. In this way, six or seven such sessions will be needed for each class.

It is recommended that as soon as possible after the conferences, brief, factual notes be written up, partly to avoid having to commit all the information to memory, and also to ensure that the head receives the benefit of the extra knowledge.

Mention was made earlier of the 5 per cent of parents who may not respond to the invitation to come in to discuss their child's growth and work programme. The wording of the invitation is very important. A suggested letter is given in Appendix A. Some schools state clearly in the letter of invitation that should it be impossible for the parents to come to school then either the head or the class teacher will very happily call round and discuss anything about which the parents are concerned in their home. In many cases this works very well, and after the first one or two visits even the most diffident teachers find the experiences extremely valuable and not half as terrifying as they had imagined.

One of the more recent developments in the field of home and school relationships has been the appointment of a teacher with a special responsibility for home visiting. I have met and talked with several of these and all are distinguished and exceptional teachers. Much of real value is accomplished by them and it may well be that this will eventually be the pattern. For myself, in some ways I rather regret this development as it seems to interpose between direct parent/teacher relationships. Even as a head who did a great deal of home visiting, I felt it was only second best for my class teachers and I persisted with it only where teachers were unable to do it themselves. If, as is sometimes argued, the teacher/social worker is really only a 'front man' who goes out solely to get parents into the school and into direct contact with the class teacher, then I support wholeheartedly this move. As yet, however, I am not convinced that this is always the case.

The setting up of conferences within the open school rounds off the steps that can be taken by any school wishing to undertake a programme of activities to promote better and wider home and school and parent/ teacher relationships. The need for 're-charging batteries', exchanging experiences, seeking help over problems, and gathering up new ideas is all that now remains. The kind of help that a school might welcome is now much more freely available through various organisations, a growing amount of literature on the subject and official encouragement. A detailed examination of all these will be found in the concluding chapters.

Chapter 7

Organisational aids

Where a school has decided to go ahead and extend its work with parents and the community, there will naturally, from time to time, be certain problems or minor crises. I can imagine that critical readers of the previous chapters might well retort 'Problems? I thought once you'd established this idea of partnership and the open school all went from strength to strength!' Inevitably, when attempting a broad review of a subject, as I am in this book, not all items of detail can be covered. To attempt, therefore, to list matters where problems or contentions might arise seems almost to invite difficulties. Certainly in any of the suggested activities and programmes snags could arise and particular local circumstances might well result in modifications becoming necessary. I would think these points would be appreciated by most. However, there would still be the legitimate query 'To whom can I turn for advice, further suggestions and positive assistance, if I come up against difficulties?'

There are three national organisations which cover the whole country in dealing with PTA questions, and one all-embracing body known as the Home and School Council. This Council contains representatives from the three national organisations, who between them must number well over two hundred thousand parents and teachers, as well as representatives from the Department of Education and Science and all the major teachers' associations.

The senior organisation, and undoubtedly the one with the most practical advice and service facilities, is the National Confederation of

Parent–Teacher Associations. This body grew partly from Susan Isaacs' and George Lyward's pre-war Home and School Council and partly from the great development of parent-teacher associations after World War Two. At first, individual school PTAs joined together for certain mutually advantageous actions. These included making specific requests to the local education authority for change within the area or region. In this way, regional federations of PTAs grew up. Sometimes these were on a county basis as in Kent or Greater London; others took in larger areas in the north-west and the Midlands. As other areas developed, so eventually there arose the idea of a national federation. The reasons for this are justified by the NCPTA itself, as follows: it can become a centre and clearing-house for ideas and can give help and advice in forming a PTA; if a school has a problem the NCPTA has access to the Secretary of State for Education, local authorities, teachers' organisations etc., this being a result of work over a number of years in building up confidence in the Federation; it can produce attractive literature and publish twice yearly a good quality magazine *The Parent-Teacher*, copies of which are sent to every country in the world. The NCPTA provides a headquarters for the PTA movement in Britain and is contacted by the British Council, government agencies and departments as well as by many visitors from abroad. Besides putting points of view through the various media when educational matters are in the news, it constantly strives to bring the work of PTAs before the public: close contact is made with teachers' organisations, whose representatives sit on the Executive Committee; an annual conference is held at which leading educationalists are invited to speak and where resolutions concerning local authorities are debated and, if agreed, passed to the authorities concerned. In all of these things the NCPTA speaks as a national body and is therefore often more effective than if actions were taken on an association basis locally.

It does seem as if the NCPTA is one of the national bodies which really does succeed in fulfilling its aims. If a school decides that it should form a parent-teacher association as one of the ways in which to achieve a better home and school relationship, then undoubtedly membership of the NCPTA will give worthwhile additional backing and help.

Recently it has introduced a valuable and very necessary comprehensive insurance cover for all subscribing members. This means a school can be relieved of all the business and worry of taking out separate policies each time a fête or fair or other function involving parents and teachers is held. A further interesting development in the scope and range of its work has been in joining with European and other national parent-teacher organisations for the exchange of information and the holding of international conferences. Certainly no school need feel it is working in isolation if it joins the NCPTA, and since the feeling of isolation can so often be the most discouraging factor in a school's growth, the Confederation plays an exceptionally important role.

The Advisory Centre for Education (Cambridge) and the Confederation of Associations for the Advancement of State Education both have different beginnings and fulfil slightly different roles. Both ACE and CASE can, however, be of real value to a school and its teachers and parents if they choose to make use of their particular services.

The Advisory Centre's Director, Brian Jackson, writes in its publication *1960–1970 A Progress Report,*

'The Centre is a voluntary body, registered as an educational charity and governed by an independent Council of which the Chairman is Dr. Michael Young, the chief mover in its creation. Its income derives from the sale of its services, chiefly the magazine *Where,* together with earmarked grants from government or foundations for particular research or demonstration projects. It is supported by the subscriptions of some 23,000 individual members, though of course large numbers of others employ the other services it provides or supports.

'The Centre was launched in 1960, and in its initial phase it was very much an attempt to repeat in education the style and success of the Consumers' Association—to create a self-aware body of education "consumers" and to provide them with the independent information necessary to make better educational choices. The lone survivor of this moment in time is probably the title of the magazine: *Where*—with its suggestion of reasoned choice as key to the parent's ideal action.

'But like any plant growing and bending in search of the sunlight, the Centre has seldom been confined by its original seeding and climate. . . .

'In its first two years therefore ACE followed a deceptively simple trail which soon petered out in the dense jungles ahead. The case for an education system (or a society) in which the receivers—parent, pupil or student—played as strong a part as the dispensers —politician, administrator, teacher—was as rich as ever. After children and students, parents and the community are the great underused and undervalued asset in the education system. They nurture the child, they provide the home background, which is the chief influence on a child's growth, they vote and fund the system itself, they have the capacity to bring into the school extra material resources, extra assistance, extra experiences, extra ideas. And at no cost. As a matter of rights, dignity, motivation and community support, the case for children and parents playing a vivid role in education is ultimately unassailable.

'Nevertheless, in 1960 it was clear that this was not the actuality, nor likely to be without a good deal of hard work; research, lobbying, publicity, action. It was not going to be easy. Every square on the board was covered—by the teachers' unions, by the powers and influence of the local authorities, by the universities, by the law. It had to be expected that every initiative we took would arouse protest and hostility. And so it certainly proved to be. There was no place for the new voice, except what could be won inch by inch. ACE therefore had to redirect its energies in several distinct ways.'

And quite correctly, as Brian Jackson stated, ACE has certainly set up and provided valuable information services about the education system in general and numerous schools in particular.

But it is undoubtedly through its journal and its very distinguished contributors that much relevant research has been publicised and further research initiated.

By publishing special editions, many knowledge gaps have been filled for hard-working and time-pressed teachers. In one school the parents and I used as a textbook, for a regular discussion group over a period of two years, ACE's *Plowden for Parents* which still remains one of the best available summaries of the great report.

At another time, ACE fostered Primary School Groups and these were, through the great work by Anne Hagger at ACE, so successful that within months over seventy were in action all over the country. Following a broadcast of mine on BBC Woman's Hour another fifty schools wrote in seeking help and advice on how to run groups within their schools which would really be partnerships and not just low-level 'tolerated' PTAs. The encouraging thing about all of this was the realisation that so many wanted to develop their schools along these lines. The interesting thing was that they either lacked the know-how or felt the need for some supportive organisation.

The Advisory Centre for Education has continued to set up or help in setting up Education Shops in town and city centres; has set up the Association of Multi-Racial Playgroups; run courses for primary and secondary teachers, one of which can claim considerable success in bringing primary school teachers who are striving to implement the recommendations of the Plowden Report. This is the Annual Plowden Course Conference presided over each year by Lady Plowden. The tutor members of this course and the others who attend have acted as a national focus on the needs of primary schools today, particularly in strengthening the work of partnership with parents. The course can rightly, therefore, claim the attention of all who seek both help and encouragement in home and school matters. ACE is now extending the successful research and work of the Education Priority Areas, especially the work in Liverpool of Dr Eric Midwinter, who is now a co-director of ACE and responsible for 'Priority', a new educational centre in his city.

ACE, like CASE, has often been described as a 'middle class organisation'. Brian Jackson's retort to this is 'Absolutely. But we hope its style and record give it some claim to disseminating, far and wide, those liberal values, and that energy in pursuing them, that represent the very best of the world in which we work.'

The Centre is, therefore, an organisation which is able to keep parents and teachers well abreast of all innovations and good practice within education. As such, therefore, ACE is of use to any school trying to effect change and build up its home and school links.

The Confederation for the Advancement of State Education comes into yet another category but one which for many schools and staff can supply the machinery, literature and publicity necessary to promote the right local climate for change. There have been many areas in the country where CASE has been able to bring parents and teachers together most effectively in order to mobilise public opinion in favour of changes within schools or administration. Although perhaps the most famous of its projects have been in connection with secondary re-organisation, the whole range of schools has been covered by its many branch associations. Much good work has resulted where they have concentrated upon poor primary school buildings or where the inflexibility of a selection system needed loosening up.

The various CASE branches claim, quite correctly, to be groups of citizens, mostly parents, who are deeply interested in education. They believe that the future of the educational system depends on the public being well informed on the major issues and keenly alive to the need for improving the range and standards of educational provision in Britain. They are not bound to any political party or religious creed any more than are the NCPTA and ACE.

Local associations of CASE hold regular meetings and arrange study groups on all aspects of education. Members systematically attend meetings of local education committees; they also support any councillors or council candidates who genuinely have the interests of schools at heart. Increasingly, CASE members have taken a more active part in administration as school managers, governors and co-opted or elected members of education committees. Local branches aim to learn as much as possible about educational conditions in their own areas and then take up matters concerning their schools with local and national government. CASE was founded in order to keep local branches in touch with one another and to act as spokesman for local associations at national level, for example by deputations to the Secretary of State for Education. A journal and other useful material is published at regular intervals.

The aims of CASE are completely laudable and have been stated as:
(1) to work for the improvement and expansion of state education
(2) to collect and spread information about national and local education policy and to provide facilities for its discussion
(3) to further communication between the local education authority, parents and others interested in education.

These aims have sometimes, however, led to suspicion or even hostility from teachers. I think these dangers are over and arose perhaps from over-zealous or insensitive local members who, in probing their schools, attempted an evaluation procedure which was sometimes too crude or at other times facilely scientific. Schools are complex places and simple solutions to their problems are rarely possible and always suspect.

As I have said, it is sad that with all pioneer work it is the exceptional, in the sensational sense, instances of activities which hit the headlines, while the many other good, straightforward pieces of worthwhile work escape the spotlight. Up and down the country there are welcome signs of real co-operation between the members of CASE, ACE and the NCPTA. It is very often here, at the grassroots, that significant progress is made in furthering the growth and development of parent-teacher partnerships.

In October 1967 the national Home and School Council was established. It comprised delegates from the NCPTA, ACE and CASE, with invited members from the Department of Education and Science and leading teachers' organisations. *The Times Educational Supplement* stated, rather picturesquely, that the Council was formed 'to carry Lady Plowden's beacon from form room to front room'. In triple federatic: it was hoped that the three constituent bodies 'could shed light and dispense help upon how to unite the efforts of both parents and teachers over their children's schooling'.

In its early days it set up an action research project in the West Riding of Yorkshire and also began the publication of working papers which, it was hoped, would assist parents and teachers in their efforts.

Naturally, when three established independent bodies start trying to work together, it takes some time for them to assimilate each other's viewpoints and establish agreed priorities. Despite differences and minor crises of one kind and another it is good that the Home and School Council survives and shows signs now of becoming the truly national forum for home and school matters. Much exceptionally useful literature comes from the Council essential for any school or PTA determined to receive the maximum assistance in its work.

In whatever area or kind of school a teacher is at work, I would certainly hope that for the relatively small sum of money involved a school could be persuaded to have available for its teachers and parents all the magazines and literature published by the four bodies we have been discussing.

Naturally, the impact of this will vary from area to area, but I suggest, again from experience, that there will always be at least a few for whom this literature will provide the spur or encouragement for further actions or will suggest ways of meeting requests which pose problems for the teacher or the school.

Chapter 8

Helpful literature

In Appendix C is a reading list which will fill in many of the details needed by those who have now decided to give home and school relationships the priority advocated in this book. This is not a complete bibliography, but those who require a fuller list can obtain one from the Home and School Council. The books I have listed are some which many teachers have found valuable and practical: valuable in producing evidence in support of the case for PTAs for perusal by sceptical or wondering colleagues; practical in so far as they give down to earth instruction about such things as the two-way report, using parents as aides, conducting interviews etc.

I would like to highlight, however, a few of the now classic works and the more recent publications, in order perhaps both to whet the appetite and reinforce some of the points made in previous chapters. The method of discussing these is in no sense on order of merit lines, but merely a revisionary exercise which links us with the text.

First of all, there are two books in which Patrick McGeeney sets out fully and clearly a whole range of investigation and case studies. These studies bring a sense of reality and possibility to the whole question of how far a teacher can and should go in these matters. In the first book, *Learning Begins at Home*, McGeeney worked with Dr Michael Young, whose guiding hand and brains were behind the early work of ACE and the Home and School Council. Patrick McGeeney is, most fortunately I feel, a teacher, and writes, therefore, not from a purely theoretical angle, nor from the comparative safety of the administrator's desk. In this book he describes how an old school, in what could well be described as an Educational Priority Area, sets about a programme of activities which could lead both to an improvement in children's educational attainments and to a great degree of active co-operation between parent and teacher.

Four proposals in particular were agreed upon: an open meeting early in the term for all parents, or as many of them as would come; private talks between individual parents and the class teachers; meetings on teaching methods dealing with innovations; home visits for some parents who would not come to the school. Incidentally, the last of the four proposals was the least successful in some ways since, not unnaturally, not all members of the staff would agree to undertake these visits.

The general results were, however, all encouraging, but wisely Young and McGeeney are extremely cautious about them and urge the need for further investigations.

The interesting comments are made that:

> 'It looks as though there may be something in the syllogism of parental participation.'
> 'A rise in the level of parental encouragement augments their children's performance at school.'
> 'By involving parents in the school teachers bring about a rise in the level of parental encouragement.'

But what also comes clearly out of *Learning Begins at Home* is what Lady Plowden describes as 'the passionate but impotent interest of so many of these parents'. They genuinely wanted to help their children, but they felt inadequate. The message is, therefore, reasonably clear for us, the teachers.

Patrick McGeeney's second book *Parents are Welcome* followed naturally from the Plowden Report's recommendations that 'extensive examples of good practice in parent-teacher relations' were needed. Over thirty different schools were visited by McGeeney, ranging across England, from Cornwall to the east end of London, taking in children from nursery schools through to comprehensives. All of these schools demonstrated in varying ways how parents and teachers can co-operate to the advantage of children and school. Honestly and objectively, but not coldly and clinically, Patrick McGeeney reported on the attitudes, discovered on both sides, of defensiveness and suspicion and how it is often a long business to change them. But, as he writes,

> 'The strongest feeling which came through in the schools I visited was the excitement of teaching and learning. In educating the parents, the teachers were educating themselves. Now that the debate about the means and order of education has become public, there are bound to be increasing numbers of parents knocking on the doors of schools for an opportunity to take part. They should

be welcomed for the educational benefit of the children, the parents and the teacher.'

Laurence Green's book *Parents and Teachers: Partners or Rivals?* was the first book in England on home and school matters to be written by a practising head, and deals in an understanding way with the answers to the following parents' questions: 'What goes on in my child's school—whom do I ask, what do I ask and dare I ask?' And for teachers 'How can I get closer to parents and enlist their aid in what I am trying to teach?'

This is an intensely practical book and still relevant for the large majority of schools and parents. Perhaps since its publication there has been an increase in literature on the subject (although it is still pitifully small compared with the American list, or even those of some of our European neighbours) but a great number of the books are not practical. I have always maintained that if teachers are tired and need tips then it is not very kind either to withhold them or to induce guilt complexes in them about accepting such tips.

Laurence Green concludes his book by stating:

> 'Parents and teachers are not enemies; they should not be rivals even, but partners. As teachers we try to see things through the child's eyes; it is a logical and valuable step to try and now see through the parents'. Much of our work is wasted if they are hostile, indifferent or just plain puzzled. And when we stop learning from parents we stop learning altogether.'

In 1967 a book appeared called *Linking Home and School* which was edited by Craft, Raynor and Cohen and contained for the first time a series of important papers written around the title theme. The contributors are all exceptionally well known and distinguished educationalists and to mention Professors Bernstein, Blyth, Wiseman and Tibble and William Taylor leaves out several others equally well known. This book supplies so much that it is valuable in discussions and with its more recent companion (also edited by Maurice Craft) *Family, Class and Education* the reader is armed with evidence and authoritative views which would cope with any sceptics or questioners he might meet. I feel very strongly that even when a teacher is convinced of the validity of his actions it is very necessary that he should also be able to turn to eminent authorities for support in what he is doing. There is not a facet of the whole business of home and school relations which is not covered in a full and scholarly way by the contributors to one or other of these two books.

A very sober conclusion, written by Professor William Taylor, reinforces my point when, in writing about the difficulties of reconciling role differences between individuals and groups, he states,

> 'Recognition of these differences may be helpful in our toleration

of the failure that will attend *some* [my italics] of our efforts, and remind us of the fact that a technique that does not have its roots in an adequate theory is, in the long run, unlikely to be either helpful or enduring.'

One of the most encouraging books for teachers is written by Ronald Cave, Senior County Inspector for Cambridgeshire and the Isle of Ely. His book *Partnership for Change : Parents and Schools* contains positive statements and good examples from the 'shop floor' but also deals with the critics of the changed pattern in primary and secondary education. An obvious believer in attack being the best method of defence, Ronald Cave sets about the Black Paper boys and their fellow travellers in a very determined and realistic way. Writing of student unrest, for example, he states (in answer to the charge that it all stems from the 'revolution' in primary methods), 'My view is if some students blow their tops once they reach university, the cause is far more likely, in the majority of cases, to be found in a reaction against the formality and repression of many of our grammar schools rather than in the fact that they have been taught to think for themselves at primary level.'

Another refreshing thing about this particular book which I found welcome was that the author shows that there are some things we can perhaps learn from America, particularly in the field of parental involvement. It is very common nowadays to dismiss all American practice with a derisory shrug or to use it as a 'seven year warning device' (this being the approximate time gap between the inception of practices in living and business in the USA and our adoption of them in this country). In this book there is a sound assessment and evaluation of educational practices in the USA and Europe which can be of help to all teachers.

Ronald Cave's conclusions are again as attacking as several sections of the book :

'Much of the argument in this book has tended to the belief that many of the tasks that are either not done at all or are done inadequately by the teacher, because of lack of time or specialist knowledge, may be and should be performed by parents. Education is a preparation for the real world; the use of men and women from the outside world in counselling about career prospects or in helping solve pupils' personal problems emphasises that the sharp distinction between the professional educator and the parent should not exist in the schools of the future. Home and school co-operation is not something that may happen—it *is* happening. We would be wise to welcome and encourage this partnership for change.'

Variations upon this and the other messages will be found in the remaining books listed in Appendix C and all will usefully add to the teacher's knowledge and expertise in this important and priority field of work.

Conclusion

From the Department of Education and Science in November 1967 came *Report on Education no. 41: Parents and Teachers*; in October 1968 came *Education Survey no. 5* entitled *Parent/Teacher Relations in Primary Schools*. Both of these publications simply and unmistakably commended to all teachers the need for a long, clear look at what could be done in improving their links with the parents of the children they taught.

Both of these official statements echoed either in fact, or by implication, the Plowden Report's message which stated clearly and emphatically 'Teachers are linked to parents by the children for whom they are responsible. The triangle should be completed and a more direct relationship established between teacher and parents. Parents should be partners in more than name; their responsibilities joint instead of several.'

The Plowden Report makes it clear that this will mean extra effort (greater productivity?) and stated:

> 'We are aware that in asking them to take on new burdens we are asking what will sometimes be next to impossible. Forty children will seem enough to manage, without adding eighty fathers and mothers. Yet we are convinced that to make the effort not only adds depth to their understanding of the children, but will also bring out that support from the home which is still often latent. It has long been recognised that education is con-

cerned with the whole man; henceforth it must be concerned with the whole family.'

But it was twenty years earlier, in January 1947, that the Ministry of Education issued its first report from the Central Advisory Council for Education entitled *School and Life*. Chapter 2 of that report was headed Home and School and, perhaps surprisingly to some of our younger colleagues, these words were written twenty-five years ago.

'Most people now recognise how important it is for home and school to work together. This working together for the same thing should begin early, and the earlier the better. Parents should take the trouble to learn about the school and what it is trying to do; in return the school must take into account how the child lives at home. This means the school having relations with, and accepting a duty towards the parents of its pupils.'

A few pages on the report states the need for parents and teachers to have frequent opportunities for contact and mentions PTAs and committees but adds:

'Although associations are of great value, the best kind of co-operation between home and school springs from the attitude shown in the day-to-day life of the school; for if a parent feels welcome, his confidence is won, and once his confidence is won, he will support the teachers in what they are trying to do. It is in this way that the values which the school is setting before a child come to be understood in his home, and the better they are understood in his home, the more will the child benefit from both home and school.'

Lord James of Rusholme in giving the inaugural Herbert Read memorial lecture stated 'The effectiveness of Britain's education depends on its being supported by the family and the community.'

In 1970 Edward Short, then Minister of Education, opened the West Silvertown Primary School in East London with his interpretation of why this support was needed, when he said:

'Today parents are welcome visitors I hope to every part of the school. This is important for two reasons. First, we have learned in the last two decades that an extremely important element in a child's progress is the attitude towards his schooling of his parents. If they are interested and willing to help—not nagging, fussy and neurotic help—but genuinely anxious to be of assistance and to show interest in what the child is doing, his progress will be the greater. Secondly, there are many new methods in schools—differing profoundly from the methods used when we were children at school— that is why it is very important for the interested parent to understand them. There is a great deal to be said for schools holding regular sessions for parents to explain new methods. Parent involve-ment takes many forms—sometimes through the vehicle of a parent/teacher or home/school association. Equally effective are ad hoc arrangements to explain methods, to use the service of parents in making equipment, etc. One of the most valuable methods of parent involvement which is now to be seen in a great many schools in the country is the invitation to be present from time to time at morning assembly. This occasion, when the school meets as a community, I believe is a unique opportunity to create the sense of community between the school and the home.'

In 1969 and 1970 the National Union of Teachers and the National Association of Schoolmasters both issued special documents on 'home and school'. The NUT issued from its Executive what was called 'an approved statement' *(The NUT View on Home and School Relations, 1969)* and the NAS called what it produced a discussion paper *(Home and School, 1970)*, and not an official expression of NAS policy. Both documents contain much that is encouraging and by reading both one would be justified, as a head or class teacher, in deciding that, to undertake work of the kind generally indicated in this book would *not* conflict with Union or Association policy.

The NAS paper says 'Teachers will be especially interested in the attitudes of parents of the children they teach. These individual atti-tudes have a great effect on the child's work in school. Where parental co-operation and understanding of difficulties are obtained the child can benefit.

> 'If the parents' attitude is in conflict with the school, it is in the interests of the child that every effort should be made to change the attitude. Some teachers are wary of too close relationships with parents because they fear difficulty in reconciling views. Parents quite rightly have views of their own which they will defend against those of the teacher. . . . Parents and pupils attached greater importance to knowledge and skill to help them get a better job and were less interested in broader educational and recreational activities than were the teachers.
>
> 'The fears of teachers in this respect must be removed. Teachers must be convinced that the parents have a point of view of which account ought to be taken and that the parents who are knowledg-able about school arrangements will better understand why things are done in a particular way.'

The NUT says quite forthrightly:

> 'The Union has always fully supported the principle of home and school relationships of the fullest kind and does so now. Even before Plowden, it welcomed the support given to its policy by discoveries in the fields of sociology and linguistics which underline

the importance of the earliest years and of early admission to school. It is clear from this also that the Union would wish to see the closest co-operation between home and school.

'The Union welcomed the principle of "positive discrimination" both in its original appreciation in Plowden, and more recently in connection with the urban development programme of providing more nursery education in deprived areas. This again implies the closest possible liaison between the home and school.

'The Union does not believe that there is one, and only one, way of achieving co-operation; nor does it believe that it has a monopoly of either wisdom or responsibility in this field. Parents have a vital interest which complements, not conflicts with, the interests of teachers, and it is to the good of both, and above all of the children, that there should be full co-operation.'

If all are with us, who can be against us?

But perhaps more correctly the last words on this subject in this book should come from Lady Plowden and they are taken from a speech made to a group of parents following the publication of the Report now permanently linked with her name.

'I rather carefully said when I was talking about schools abroad that we felt what we were doing in ours was as good as anything we saw elsewhere. This did *not* however apply to the relationships between the community and parents and teachers. Here we lag behind. In Denmark, parents and neighbours went on expeditions with the schools, helped after school hours in clubs. In America parents help in the schools, both on a voluntary and paid basis in the same school.

'This source of help to the schools and the contribution has yet to be recognised in this country. I think it still has to be realised by teachers that the ultimate responsibility for the child rests with the parents and that the child will develop his full potential only if the education has the full support of the parent. To give this, the parent must be recognised as an equal partner by the teacher and must know and understand what it is the school is doing. This is just as essential whoever the parents may be, whether they are professional, or whether they are parents living in sub-standard conditions and only just managing to cope.

'This relationship calls for delicacy and tact, probably from both sides. Even though I think that parents, particularly from the less educated parts of the community, may be frightened and too anxious to approach teachers, so teachers I think may be frightened of parents, both of those who come from a different layer of society from themselves and also from professional parents. They may be frightened that professional parents will interfere, that they will try to run the school, that they will be critical of what the teachers are doing, that they will be another burden for the teacher.

'But even as we are all just ordinary people, and there are few very outstanding people among us, so are teachers. Just ordinary people, doing their job as well as they can. They will make mistakes, even as we make mistakes, but they will also deploy their skill in doing the best they can for your child. They will do better the more confidence they have—your active support will help them achieve this confidence. Once there is confidence between both these two vital influences in a child's life, the child is more likely to progress without tension. And an absence of tension is a necessity for learning. . . .'

Appendix A

Example of a letter to parents regarding interviews:

Marshlands Primary School

Dear ....,

Both parents and teachers at our school have expressed a wish for a closer relationship between school and home. I am sure that we all agree that a 'conference' between a child's teacher and his parents is one means of strengthening that relationship. I use the word 'conference' rather than 'interview' or just plain 'meeting' because 'conference' means 'a meeting for discussion and the exchanging of views'. In other words, a 'get together' of equal partners.

We are planning to start these conferences on Tuesdays between 3.00 and 4.30 p.m. and between 6.30 and 8.30 p.m. Will you please indicate your first, second and third choices on the dates listed below? At all of these times your child's teacher will be present to meet you.

Thank you.

Yours sincerely,

Head Teacher

Choice				
( )	3.00–4.30 p.m.	Tuesday	9th Feb.
( )	3.00–4.30 p.m.	,,	16th Feb.
( )	3.00–4.30 p.m.	,,	23rd Feb.
( )	6.30–8.30 p.m.	,,	9th Feb.
( )	6.30–8.30 p.m.	,,	16th Feb.
( )	6.30–8.30 p.m.	,,	23rd Feb.

N.B. We shall allocate approximately thirty minutes for each conference.

Example of Prospectus

Buckskin County Junior School

The school was opened in May 1965 and is built to accommodate 480 children. For the next few years we may well have considerably more than that number of children and extra temporary accommodation has been provided by the County Education Officer.

Children normally enter the school at approximately 7½ years of age and stay for a four year course leaving us at eleven years of age to go on to Secondary Schools.

In each of the four year groups there are formed three or four classes. Each of these classes within a year group is equal in every way. This means that we are an 'unstreamed' school and the children are *not* segregated according to ability. This further means that within each class most of the day's work is on an individual or group basis. The groups within a class vary according to the activity being carried out. There are no bells rung between lessons since sometimes pupils and staff who are really engrossed upon some work activity may continue with it uninterrupted. The teachers' job is to encourage, help and see that over the period of the day or week every child in the room covers the right balance of varied work.

All of this is very different from most of our own ideas of school work but I can assure you *it produces* good results and happy children and has the official approval of the Department of Education.

We would like you as parents to learn how we work and then assist us in this work. You can only learn *how* we work by visiting us regularly. This is also new and strange for some of you but we genuinely mean our invitation. Drop into school regularly. Get to know, *really know*, your child's teacher. When this happens your child's rate of progress will be anything up to 25% better. (This has been proved by educational research.)

How You Can Help Us (and your child). **Please:**

1. See that your child attends school regularly and punctually (this is still important!). If absent a visit or written message or 'phone call is needed from you.

2. There is no school uniform and I welcome variety of dress and colours but all clothes should be practical. A boy or girl wants to feel comfortable if they are to work well and not have to worry unduly about their clothes.

3. An apron, overall or smock for boys and girls is essential if they are to really enjoy their Art and Craft lessons.

4. P.T. shoes (black or white), *white* vest or singlet or T. shirt and *black* shorts for Physical Education. For all boys football boots are desirable but not vitally necessary in the first year classes. A strong pair of old shoes for football would be suitable rather than that they should kick the toes out of their proper shoes. Boys are told which afternoon their Games lessons take place. Black football socks with white tops *if* you are buying specially.

Swimming will be taken by more classes when the new West Ham Pool is opened. At present it has to be limited to our 4th Year Juniors.

5. Let them use the Central County Children's Library and the School Library. Books of all kinds are vital at this stage for every child's development and progress and not just for the so-called 'brainy' child. I include magazines and 'comics' in my definition of books. If time can be found it is *still* a good idea to read to your child—the traditional '10 minute' read when tucked up in bed is excellent.

Also to hear your child read to you regularly is a great help at all stages of Junior education.

6. All clothing (including footwear) should be marked—and re-marked at intervals —with your boy's or girl's names.

7. Let them have the free daily milk but if you do not wish this a written message from you is necessary.

8. All children may stay to the midday meal which is properly balanced and of the correct calorie content. It is very helpful if these are paid for weekly on Monday mornings.

9. No official homework may be set and this is in accordance with the County Council rules but if you visit your child's teacher regularly there are many useful activities that may be suggested by the teacher from time to time for your child to do at home. Television lessons are taken in school and if parents are able to follow those taken by their child it is a good thing to talk about these together and do follow up work together at home.

10. No child is ever kept in after school hours unless you have been informed on the previous day. No corporal punishment is permitted in school.

11. All educational visits, special or early closures are always notified to you in writing. A list of holiday dates for the year is always sent home but they can also be seen at any time on the notice board in the lower Main Corridor.

Educational visits are a definite feature of our work programme and your support in these visits by contributions towards the cost, by offering occasionally to accompany the children and generally taking an interest in the trips will be specially welcomed.

12. If anything is lost at school do let us have details and *make sure* that your child has told the School Secretary as well as the class teacher.

13. All subjects are compulsory for all children except Religious Instruction and attendance at Assemblies. Any child *for any reason* may be excused Religious Instruction or Assemblies simply by the parent writing a straightforward request. No reason needs to be given. A note requesting temporary excusing on medical grounds from physical education is normally valid for only one week.

14. Written Reports are issued once a year only but at any time the Head or Class Teacher will gladly give a verbal report. The written Report is in two parts and on the second part we invite you to add your comments, suggestions and any further information.

15. *Always* ask if you have any queries or worries however small or large regarding your child's education. Remember that so often the seemingly small things are vitally important. We welcome your interest and visits.

16. Monthly meetings are held in School of our 'Primary School Group' made

Parent-teacher Partnership

up of Parents and Teachers to discuss the Plowden Report on Primary Education and to see how we can make its recommendations work here in Buckskin. Special General Meetings of parents are held to hear outside speakers, to discuss particular activities or to plan social events. Please come along to as many of these as you are able.

17. Lessons in Road Safety are given regularly and with the help of the Road Safety Officer and Police and *your* active support the accident rate can be cut. Cycle Training and Testing classes are held every term.

All boys and girls are encouraged to join the Schools' Trustee Savings Bank Scheme.

18. A list of Staff names and their classes and session times is sent home at the beginning of each School Year in September and may also be found on the Parents' Notice Board in the Lower Corridor. School Newsletters are also sent home throughout the year.

GRAHAM BOND

Headmaster.

Example of Newsletter: Prior Weston Primary School

NEWSLETTER No. 9

This last term has been the busiest since we opened in September 1968. We have had three School Journeys, with parties of children in Dorset (15 days), Sussex (4 days) and Norfolk (5 days). This meant that seventy-four children had the opportunity of spending some time away from home (an undoubted benefit to parents and offspring alike). Next year we hope to repeat our Sussex visit and send a group of 2nd and 3rd year juniors to North Devon. If you have a child in this age range (9+–10+) and have not received details please ask Mrs Tipple for the relevant letters.

The various PTA meetings have been very well supported and an equally interesting and varied programme is being prepared for next term. I would particularly draw your attention to the meeting on Tuesday, 12th October at 8.00 p.m. when Guy Rogers, ILEA, Inspector for Secondary Education will talk on 'Secondary Schools'. This is a topic which concerns us all—even if little John is only five now he will eventually enter a secondary school . . . what then?

May I end on a purely administrative note. It may be that when your child returns to school next term the teaching areas will be somewhat different: simply put, the present Upper School block housing the Lower School children and vice versa. This is purely to obtain maximum space per child with the existing build-ing. It does not mean that because of exceptional progress and brilliant teaching all the younger ones have gone up and (for the opposite reasons) all the older ones have gone down. Finally a quiet voice in my ear reminds me that in any case our children go neither up nor down—only across!

H.P.

Summer Club

The Lower School Summer Club is now fully booked and no further children can be accepted.

52

Out and About

Children have made visits to the following places of interest:

St. James' Park	St. Paul's Cathedral
Covent Garden Market	Horniman's Museum
Tower of London	Highgate Ponds
Science Museum	Museum of Natural History
St. Magnus the Martyr Church	City Bridges and river visits
Guildhall and Museum	Hadley Woods
St. John's Gate and Clerkenwell	Barbican show flats

New Faces

Miss Eleanor Morton joins the staff in September and will work in the Lower School. Eleanor has been in and out of school since last November so she will be no stranger to most of you.

To foster music in the school, Mrs. Margot Eagan has been appointed on a part time basis.

Both teachers are additional to the staff we already have.

Crossing Patrol

We now have permission to have a crossing patrol in Golden Lane (mornings and afternoons only). Is there any parent who would be able to spare the time to do this simple but essential job? The financial reward might be microscopic but if one child is saved from injury . . . . Could you help?

Holiday Dates

	School closes	School re-opens
Christmas	22nd Dec '71	5th Jan '72
Half Term	18th Feb	28th Feb
Easter	28th March	17th April
Half Term	26th May	5th June
Summer	21st July	4th Sept
Half Term	20th Oct	30th Oct

A group of 26 children went to Norfolk . . . .

OUR SCHOOL JOURNEY TO NORFOLK

We went to Norfolk by train, it was a two hour journey. When we arrived at Kings Lynn a school bus was waiting to take us to Snettisham School. On the way to school we stopped at a pig farm and the pigs were much bigger than I thought. Then we arrived at Snettisham School where we were introduced to the people we were going to stay with. The next day we went to Cackley Clay, it was very old. We walked over the drawbridge and we saw a long hut and the Iceni Chiefs hut and a Round house. On Wednesday we went to The Broads. We had lunch on a boat and we saw some greylag geese. On Thursday we went to The Royal Norfolk Show. We saw a horse jumping show while we had our lunch, then me and the girl I stayed with got lost but we soon found the teachers. Then we saw a cow being milked and the next day. We went to Kings Lynn and came home on a train again.

Theresa Page   (aged seven)

A group of 30 children went to Weymouth . . . .

THE WAR

The sea declares war
with the pebbles
    on Chesil beach

It swells up an army
and pounces
    on Chesil beach

But then it retreats
to its salty home
    on Chesil beach

But as it retreats
it pulls some pebbles
as prisoners from their brothers
    on Chesil beach

So they roar and roar
and crackle and slide
    on Chesil beach

But the sea cares little
for all these pebbles
it just crashes down
    on Chesil beach

And pulls
    on Chesil beach

It pulls the pebbles down
into its salt drenched home
    on Chesil beach

Did you know before
you read this that
there is a constant war
going on between the pebbles
and the sea
    on Chesil beach?

Irene Endicott   (aged $10\frac{1}{2}$).

18 children went to Chichester camping . . . .

EARTHAM WOOD

The students came and took us to Eartham Wood. We found on decaying tree trunks some yellow fungus that looked like a yellow flower with no stem. Also we found some green and orange fungi. After that we went to Arundel Castle. If a castle can be beautiful, this castle surely is. We saw the keep and other rooms in the castle. We saw the place where the food is stored, and one part of the castle which is not open to the public, it has a private swimming pool. I used up all my film there. In the evening we walked to Chichester Channel by footpaths and then back to Chichester by the main road. We walked at least 4 miles.

Jonathan Miller   (aged 9 years).

The PTA Secretary writes:—

Our several parent evenings were as usual very well attended. The two maths evenings made us all use our brains and the talk from Mr. Braide proved very lively with some real audience participation.

The Summer Draw has progressed well under the capable hands of Alan Page (winning numbers below). As you are aware the aim is an extension to the school so we will have to work hard for some time to come.

The Summer Club will be run again this August. The staff will be supported by various parents, whom I will thank in advance. This Club received a marvellous boost with a generous donation from the Corporation of London, which has enabled us to purchase equipment and toys. We have also managed to get hold of other various outside equipment so the children will be well provided for—and of course the equipment is permanent.

Finally a number of our children leave this term and we wish them well in their new schools.

Barbara Boyden.

Winning Numbers

1st prize	No. 1955	S. Ames—Hornchurch.
2nd prize	No. 4259	
3rd prize	No. 598	Jackie MacKenzie, 49 Bayer House.
4th prize	No. 5656	F. G. Goynson, Walker & Rice Ltd., Q. Victoria St., EC4
Book tokens		
	No. 134	Colin Brown, Smithfield Tavern.
	No. 5028	L. Hall, 44 Bayer House.
	No. 3187	Henry P. Gormally.
	No. 5285	Stephanie Page, 56 Basterfield House.
	No. 3727	L. T. Mick, "Chequers" Old Street.
	No. 2171	Mrs. D'Mello.
	No. 3366	Mrs. Gladstone.
	No. 5360	M. Regan, Hall Keepers Off, Guildhall.
	No. 814	Mrs. A. McGiffin, 3B, Gadderstene House.
	No. 1272	Mrs. Y. Tebbutt, St. Leonard's Nursery.

Example of parents' information sheet   Prior Weston Primary School

GETTING READY FOR SCHOOL

This was prepared for parents as a direct result of a group meeting. Many of the points made below are very obvious—but if you don't understand some of the finer points (particularly those under 'Suggestions') please come in and ask for clarification. The teaching staff are here to help you!

General

1)   Bring your child to school before he starts full time schooling. We do not have a set plan for parents to follow—but a rough guide would be for children to be brought to school at least 12 times in the term before he reaches 5, and on half a dozen occasions before this. The visit need not be a long one— half an hour is often sufficient for a $4\frac{1}{4}$ year old. Stay with your child so that he can understand that school is not a place which separates children from their parents. Remember to visit during morning and afternoon sessions so that your child can have a variety of school experiences (stories, playing with structural apparatus, P.E. etc.).

2)   Try to make sure (if you live locally) that your child knows his way to and from school and can cope with the roads.

Practical

How helpful it would be if all children coming new to school could do the following things:—

1)   Tie shoelaces
2)   Dress and undress
3)   Remove outdoor clothing and hang them on a hanger
4)   Use a knife and fork
5)   Use the toilet properly
6)   Wash and dry hands and face efficiently
7)   Tidy up after using toys, apparatus, books.

Points 1–7 are, of course, aspects of social training which are as vital to teachers as to parents.

Suggestions

1)   Include your child in adult conversations whenever practical. Never talk down to him. Discuss arrangements for shopping, holiday, trips and so on with him. Watch television together and discuss the programme items—Blue Peter, How, Magpie, Jackanory, Play School are particularly suitable.
2)   Read to your child—every day if possible. Take your child to the public library and encourage him to look at books.
3)   Make scrap books with pictures. Print relevant words beneath each picture. *Never* print in capitals. These scrap books may then be used as simple reading books.
4)   Introducing reading. We have no formal scheme in school but the Ladybird series is very suitable for use at home—Books 1a, 2a, 3a, 4a.

5)   Encourage your child to paint, crayon, cook—activities which give opportunity for conversation and increase confidence.

6)   Play games with your child which encourage counting or recognition of shapes e.g. Ludo, Snakes and Ladders, Snap, Jigsaws.

7)   Help your child to realise how numbers occur in life—not by doing sums but by counting in various ways (e.g. How many forks on the table? How many cars in the road?). Number rhymes and songs also are a great help.

8)   Make use of the opportunities provided by local nursery schools and play groups.

When your child eventually begins school he will be placed in a 'family grouped' unit, i.e. there will be an age spread from 5 to 7+. When he is 8+ (a second year junior) he will move into a single age group for a year. The last two years in school (9+, 10+) are once more 'family grouped'.

Appendix B

Addresses of Organisations

Advisory Centre for Education—Cambridge
32, Trumpington St., Cambridge CB2 1QY

Confederation of Associations for the Advancement of State Education
81, Rustlings Rd., Sheffield 511 7AB

Home and School Council
81, Rustlings Rd., Sheffield 511 7AB

National Confederation of Parent-Teacher Associations
1, White Avenue, Northfleet, Gravesend, Kent

Pre-School Playgroups Association
87a Borough High St., London, SE1

Priority
Harrison Jones School
West Derby St., Liverpool 7

Appendix C

Home and School Reading List

Bailard & Strang	*Parent-Teacher Conferences* (McGraw-Hill)
Barnes, Britton & Rosen	*Language, the Learner and the School* (Penguin)
Blackie, J.	*Inside the Primary School* (Department of Education and Science)
Bloom, Davis & Hess	*Compensatory Education for Cultural Deprivation* (Holt, Reinhart & Winston)
Blyth, W. A. L.	*English Primary Education*, Vols. 1 and 2 (Routledge & Kegan Paul)
Cave, R.	*Partnership for Change: Parents and Schools* (Ward Lock Education)
Craft, M.	*Family, Class and Education* (Longman)
Craft, Raynor & Cohen	*Linking Home and School* (Longman)
Deutsch, M.	*The Disadvantaged Child and the Learning Process* (Columbia University Press)
Douglas, J. W. B.	*The Home and School* (Panther: McGibbon & Kee)
Evans, K. M.	*Attitudes and Interests in Education* (Routledge & Kegan Paul)
Eyken, Willem	*The Pre-School Years* (Penguin)
Floud, Halsey & Martin	*Education, Economy and Society* (Free Press, U.S.A.)
Fraser, Elizabeth	*Home Environment and the School* (University of London Press)
Goodacre, Elizabeth	*School and Home* (National Foundation for Educational Research)

Green, Laurence	*Parents and Teachers: Partners or Rivals?* (Allen & Unwin)
Heffernann & Todd	*Elementary Teachers' Guide to Working with Parents* (Parker, New York)
Hummelweit, H. T.	*Socio-Economic Background and Personality* (UNESCO)
Jackson & Marsden	*Education and the Working Class* (Routledge & Kegan Paul)
Jackson, Brian	*Streaming—an Education System in Miniature* (Routledge & Kegan Paul)
Lane, Homer	*Talks to Parents and Teachers* (Allen & Unwin)
McGeeney, P.	*Parents are Welcome* (Longman)
McGeeney & Young	*Learning Begins at Home: A Study of a Junior School and its Parents* (Routledge & Kegan Paul)
March & Abrams	*The Education Shop* (A.C.E.)
Musgrove & Taylor	*Society and the Teacher's Role* (Routledge & Kegan Paul)
Niemeyer	*Home-School Interactions in Relation to Learning in the Elementary School* (National Education Association, Washington)
Oeser, O. A.	*Teacher, Pupil and Task* (Tavistock)
Poster, Cyril	*The School and the Community* (Macmillan)
Pringle, Butler & Davis	*Eleven Thousand Seven Year Olds* (Longman)
Saltsmann, H.	*The Community School in the Urban Setting* (Columbia University Press)
Sharrock, Anne	*Home/School Relations* (Macmillan)
Wiseman, S.	*Education and Environment* (Manchester University Press)
Yardley, Alice	*Exploration and Language* (Evans)

In addition the following Government Reports should be studied since constant reference to them is made by many writers and speakers on Home and School matters:—

Half Our Future   Newsom
Children and Their Primary Schools, Vols. 1 and 2   Plowden
Primary Education in Wales   Gittins
The Needs of New Communities   Cullingworth (Ministry of Housing and Local Government)

Index